2nd Grade
Hooked on Phonics®
Word Games

Copyright © 2007 Educate Products, LLC. All rights reserved.
Printed in China. No part of this publication may be reproduced, stored in any retrieval system or transmitted, in any form or by any means, electronic, mechanical, photocopying, recording, or otherwise, without the prior written permission of the publisher.

© 2007 Educate Products, LLC

Hooked on Second Grade *Super Workbook*

Cleanup Time

Slam and Dunk need to do a few chores. Unscramble the letters under each picture. Then write the word below. Use the word box if you need help.

| cook | mop | sweep | wash |

peswe

_____

haws

_____

koco

_____

pmo

_____

Fun in the Sun

Circle six action words that describe what everyone is doing in the park.

Word Scramble

Today is Dunk's birthday!
Slam is telling him to do something.
Unscramble the letters in each word. Then write the words on the lines. What is Slam telling Dunk to do?

EMAK A SHIW

___ ___ ___

Who Has It?

The monkey has lost his banana. Help Detective Dog find out who has it.

Look at the pictures. Draw a line to match each picture with its word. Then write the first letter of each word on the lines below. This will tell who has the banana!

   swim

   nap

   add

   kiss

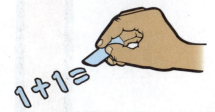   eat

___ ___ ___ ___ ___

Having Fun

Detective Dog likes to solve mysteries. Slam and Dunk like to ride skateboards for fun. What do you like to do? Draw a picture of something you do to have fun.

Write down what you like to do.
Complete the sentences below. Use the words in the word box for ideas.

At the playground, I like to _____.

At the beach, I like to _____.

At school, I like to _____.

When it snows, I like to _____.

Most of all, I like to _____.

hide	find	play
read	sled	swim
swing	talk	walk

Missing Things

Detective Dog's friend is missing a few things. Look at the pictures of the things that are missing. Then read the note. Make a list of the four things that are missing.

Dear Detective Dog,

I am taking a trip, but I cannot find some things I need. I have lost my comb. I cannot find my soap or my toothbrush.

My mirror is gone too. I hope you can help me find these things. I need to pack my suitcase. Please help!

Your friend, Fox

1. _____ 2. _____

3. _____ 4. _____

Things That Rhyme

Use the words in the box to finish the poem. Be sure to make the poem rhyme. Read the poem out loud when you are done!

My friend is a mouse.

He lives in a _____.

His friend is a cat.

She has a red _____.

Her friend is a bear.

He is eating a _____.

Sound Alikes

Some words look alike but mean different things. Look at the pictures. Then read the sentences below. Circle the sentence that best matches the picture.

Slam sheds a tear.

Slam tears up a letter.

Dunk likes to watch television.

This is a gold watch.

What Am I?

There are many animals at the zoo.
Read each clue. Then write the name of the animal next to the sentence.

lion   monkey   snake   zebra

I slither and hiss. I am a _____.

I can swing from a tree. I am a _____.

I am king of the cats. I am a _____.

I have stripes. I am a _____.

At the Beach

Help Detective Dog find all the things that belong on the beach.
This is a game for two players.

You will need:
3 coins

How to play:

1. Each player takes a coin to use as a playing piece. One person is heads. The other is tails.

2. Put both coins on START. The first player flips the third coin.

3. If the coin lands on tails, the player moves one space. If the coin lands on heads, the player moves two spaces.

4. If the player lands on a space with something you do at the beach, he acts out the sentence. If the player lands on something that you do not do at the beach, he goes back a space.

5. Take turns until both players get to the beach.

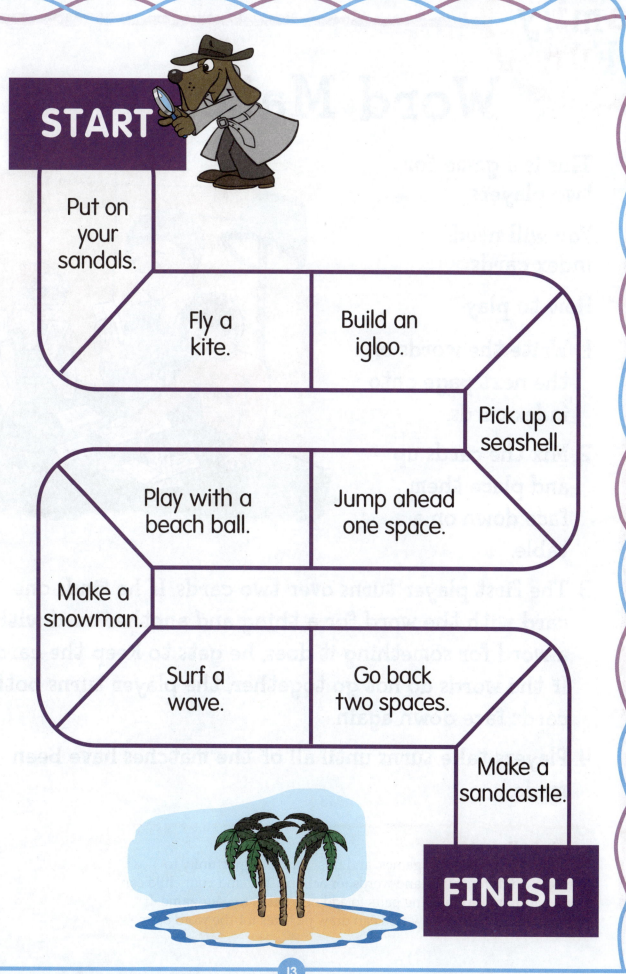

Word Match

This is a game for two players.

You will need: index cards

How to play:

1. Write the words on the next page onto index cards.

2. Mix the cards up and place them face down on a table.

3. The first player turns over two cards. If he finds one card with the word for a thing and another card with a word for something it does, he gets to keep the cards. If the words do not go together, the player turns both cards face down again.

4. Players take turns until all of the matches have been made.

Note to Parents
Children love matching games, and this is a fun opportunity to review words for things and words for actions. You and your child can brainstorm more matching pairs to add new cards to your game. If your child prefers to draw, you can draw pictures for the word pairs.

rabbit	hop
fish	swim
monkey	swing
horse	gallop
dog	bark
bird	fly

It's a Party!

Slam and Dunk want to invite all their friends to a party. Help them write the invitation. Circle all the words that should begin with a capital letter.

dear bobcat,

slam and dunk are having a party! please come! the party will be held on tuesday, june 10, at 3 o'clock at 109 river road in greentown.

see you there!

slam and dunk

Capital Idea

I did it!

Detective Dog gave his notebook to a friend, but he cannot remember which friend! Complete each sentence below. Use a capital letter to begin every sentence. Also use a capital letter when you write the name of a month or a day of the week.

| America | March | lions | Sunday |

The day that comes after Saturday is _____.

_____ live in the jungle.

The United States of _____ is a country.

The month that comes before April is _____.

Now draw a circle around each of the capital letters that you wrote. Write the capital letters in the same order in the spaces below. This will tell who has Detective Dog's notebook.

____ ____ ____ ____

Play Ball!

Read the story. Write the word that best fits in each blank space. Remember that names of people, places, and days of the week start with capital letters.

| Beth | everyone | main |
| Marie | Monday | street |

Slam and Dunk played a basketball game on _____ afternoon. They played on teams with two girls, _____ and _____. The court was in a gym on _____ _____. Slam and Beth played a good game, and so did Dunk and Marie. _____ had fun.

What Day Is It?

Read the clues below. Then write the answer to each question. Use the calendar to help you. Remember, days of the week start with capital letters.

OCTOBER						
SUNDAY	MONDAY	TUESDAY	WEDNESDAY	THURSDAY	FRIDAY	SATURDAY
1	2	3	4	5	6	7
8	9	10	11	12	13	14
15	16	17	18	19	20	21
22	23	24	25	26	27	28
29	30	31				

1. It is the first day of the week. What day is it?

   _____

2. It is the day before Friday. What day is it?

   _____

3. It is the day after Monday. What day is it?

   _____

4. October 31 is a holiday. What holiday is it?

   _____

Pen Pals

Slam wrote you a letter! Read the letter and write one back! Remember that months, days of the week, and names of people and places all begin with a capital letter.

From the Desk of

SLAM

Dear Friend,

　　How are you? I am fine.
My best friend is Dunk. We love to play basketball and other sports. My favorite month of the whole year is July.
My favorite day of the week is Sunday.
I love ice cream and skateboarding.
What do you like to do? Write back and tell me!

　　　　　　　　　　Your friend,

　　　　　　　　　　Slam

From the Desk of

_____

Dear Slam,

    It was nice to read your letter. I like to _____. My best friend is _____. My favorite month is _____. I live in a town called _____. My favorite day of the week is _____.

                              Your friend,

                              _____

A Fun Lunch

Use the pictures to help you read the story. Then fill in the missing quotation marks. Remember that quotation marks (" ") are used to show what someone is saying.

The ☀ was shining. It was time for lunch, but 🐻 and 🦊 wanted to do something that would make them 🙂.

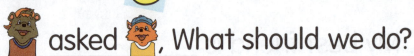
🐻 asked 🦊, What should we do?

🦊 replied, Let's have a picnic.

🐻 asked, What should we bring?

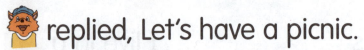
🦊 said, Let's bring some 🍞 and a jar of 🍯!

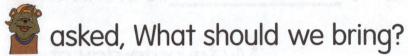
Then 🐻 had an idea. Let's sit on my 🟫!

They packed up their 🛒 and went to the park. 🐻 and 🦊 put the 🟫 on the grass and had a picnic lunch. They felt 🙂.

🦊 told 🐻, This was a great idea!

Best Bike in Town

Use the words in the word box to finish the poem. Then read the poem out loud. Be sure to include quotation marks.

"Hello"   "Cool!"

I have a new red bicycle.

I rode it to my school.

When I said _____ to all my pals,

They saw me and said, _____

The Missing Sneakers

Detective Dog's friend Rabbit sent him a letter. The letter is missing periods, commas, question marks, and exclamation points. Help Detective Dog read the letter by filling in the punctuation marks.

Dear Detective Dog ▢

My shoes are missing ▢ I had them in the park ▢ Now they are gone ▢ Do you think that the park is a good place to look ▢ I asked my friend Duck if he had seen them ▢ but he said no ▢ Maybe my friends Fox ▢ Pig ▢ and Bug can help too ▢

Your friend ▢

Rabbit

Make a Note of It!

I did it!

Detective Dog wrote some notes about a mystery.

Help finish the notes by adding periods, commas, question marks, and exclamation points.

, . ? !

I need to ask Rabbit a few questions

Where is the park

Are his shoes red white or blue

What size are they

How old are the shoes

There is no time to lose

Finish That Story!

Read the story. Then help finish it!

Detective Dog was going to the park. On the way, he saw his friend Duck.

"What is wrong?" Detective Dog asked.

"I lost my socks," said Duck.

"I did not think that ducks wore socks," said Detective Dog.

"These are special socks," said Duck.

What else will Detective Dog and Duck say to each other? How will the story end?

Finish writing the story.

_____

_____

_____

_____

_____

_____

When you are done writing, check your work for capital letters, periods, question marks, commas, and quotation marks. Read your story to a friend!

Mark the Spot

Read the story on the next page with a family member. Read each sentence. Think about how it sounds. At the end of each sentence, write a ?, ., or !. Read the whole story together when you are finished.

Note to Parents
As you read the story aloud, be sure to add dramatic effect. This will emphasize how punctuation affects the meaning of a sentence and the way it should be read.

Put the right punctuation mark at the end of each sentence.

> ?   .   !

I have a great story to tell you __

My friend and I found buried treasure __

Where do you think we found it __

It was at the park __

First we saw a gold coin. Then we saw another __

How many do you think we found __

We found a treasure chest __

My friend said, "We are rich __"

I said, "Can you believe it __"

Which Word?

Circle the word that matches each picture.

quiet loud   young old   empty full

sad happy   asleep awake   fast slow

Riddle Time

Help solve Detective Dog's riddle.

Look at each word. Find a word in the word box that means the same thing as that word. Write the word in the boxes. Then read the red boxes going down to find the answer.

What does a house wear?

over

messy

father

storm

simple

little

nap

above   dad   dirty
easy   rain   sleep   small

Opposite or the Same?

Read the clues. Then use the words in the word box to complete the puzzle.

> down   far   neat   quick   sick   under

Across:

1. This word means the same as "ill."

3. This word means the same as "below."

6. This word means the same as "clean."

Down:

2. This word means the opposite of "slow."

4. This word means the opposite of "up."

5. This word means the opposite of "near."

Word Match

Look at each picture. Find the word in the word box that describes the picture. Write the word next to the picture. Then draw a line to the word that means the opposite.

| clean | glad | noisy | quick |

_____

messy

_____

sad

_____

slow

_____

quiet

True or False?

Read each sentence. Make the sentence true by replacing the red word with a word from the word box. Write the new word on the line.

open	dry	good
sad	tall	under

Slam is happy that he spilled milk on the floor.

_____

It is a bad day at the beach.

_____

Dunk set the blocks in a very short stack.

_____

Detective Dog's umbrella helps him stay wet.

_____

The mouse is over the bed.

_____

The bird flew through the closed window.

_____

Picture Pairs

Make a book about things that are the same and things that are opposite.

Write the word "same" on five pieces of paper and the word "opposite" on five more pieces.

Find pictures in magazines or newspapers that you can put on each page.

Staple your book together and show it to your family.

Ask what is the same about the things on the pages marked "same" and why the things on the pages marked "opposite" are different from each other.

Make That Match!

This is a game for two or more players.

You will need:

index cards

full	hard	hot	near
over	slow	up	young

How to play:

1. Write the words in the word box on the index cards.
2. Put the cards into a hat or bowl.
3. The first player chooses a card. He reads the word on the card to himself. Then he thinks of a word that is the opposite of the word on the card. He tells the opposite word to the other players.
4. The other players try to guess the word on the card.
5. Each player takes turns until all of the cards have been used.

Note to Parents
Playing games such as "Make That Match" helps your child expand his vocabulary and develop critical thinking skills. Be sure to give your child the time he needs to think up an opposite word.

Happy Birthday!

Some words are spelled the same but mean different things. Fill in the poem's missing words. Use the words in the word box to help you. You will need to use each word twice.

| bark   play   rock |

I got many gifts for my birthday—

A brand new violin to _____,

A boat that can _____ in the breeze,

And a keyboard with shiny new keys.

I got a puppy that likes to _____,

And a ball to _____ with in the park.

I got some funny gifts too, you see.

A few leaves and _____ from a tree.

Plus a turtle and a pair of socks.

But my favorite is a big gray _____.

Fun at the Fair

Read the story below.
Then look at each picture. Write the word for each thing on the line below its picture.

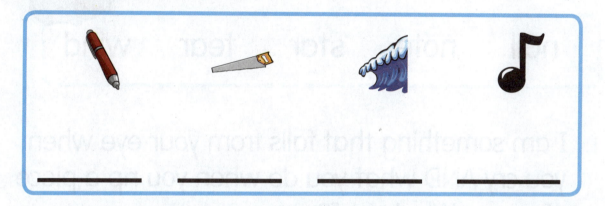

___ ___ ___ ___

Yesterday my family went to the fair. We saw cows and sheep kept inside a . Then we a band play on a stage. We clapped when they finished, and they all took a bow. At the end of the show, we saw the performers goodbye. When I got home, I wrote my friend a to tell her all about my day!

What Am I?

Help Detective Dog solve these riddles. Write the answer to each riddle on the line. Use the words in the word box to help you.

| nail | note | star | tear | wind |

1. I am something that falls from your eye when you cry AND what you do when you rip a piece of paper. What am I? _____

2. I am something you play on a piano AND something you write to your friend. What am I? _____

3. I am something that shines in the sky at night AND someone with a big part in a movie. What am I? _____

4. I am something on the end of your finger AND something that you hammer. What am I? _____

5. I am something that you do to a toy AND something that blows through the air. What am I? _____

Mix and Match

Find the word in the word box that matches both pictures in each row. Write the word on the line.

| tear | watch | wind |

_____

_____

 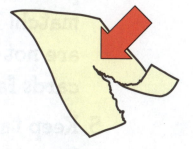

_____

Look-Alike Match

This is a game for two players.

You will need:

index cards

How to play:

1. Each word on the next page has two meanings. Draw two pictures for each word onto index cards. On the first index card, draw a picture of one meaning of the word. On the second index card, draw the other meaning of the word. Do this for every word on page 43. You should have 10 pairs or 20 cards.

2. Mix up the cards and place them face up on a table. Players should study where the cards are.

3. Then turn all the cards face down.

4. The first player turns over one card and tries to remember where the matching card is. He turns over another card. Are the words for the pictures spelled the same? If they are, it is a match! The player keeps the cards. If the words are not spelled the same, the player turns both cards face down. It is the next player's turn.

5. Keep taking turns until all the matches have been made.

tear	pen
saw	nail
play	bat
bark	note
wave	bow

New Sneakers

Slam and Dunk have written a story, but they are not sure which words to use.

Heel, heal, and he'll sound alike but have different meanings.

> Heel is the back part of your foot.
> Heal means to get healthy or well.
> He'll is a shorter way to say "he will."

Read the story. Circle the best word for each choice.

Slam and Dunk are playing basketball. Slam is wearing new sneakers. He ties the laces too tight, and he gets a blister on his (he'll/heel)! (Heal/He'll) have to stop playing for today so his (heel/he'll) can (heel/heal). Slam really likes to play, so (he'll/heal) be very happy when his foot is better!

What Should We Do?

Write the missing words to finish the poem. Look at the pictures in the box to help you. The pictures sound like the missing words, but they are not spelled the same.

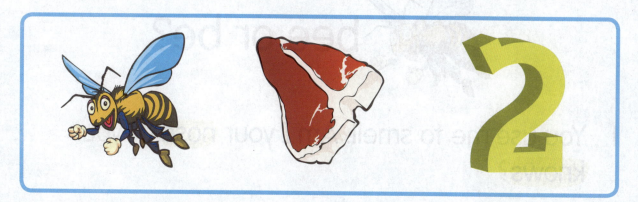

What do you want to do today?

Should we go outside and play?

There will _____ a parade and things to eat.

There will be a lot to see and people to _____.

Slam and Dunk will be there _____.

Tell me, what would you like to do?

Riddle Time

Help solve these riddles.
Read each clue. Circle the answer for each one.

bee or be?

1. You use me to smell. Am I your **nose** or your **knows**?

2. I help a boat move. Am I a **sale** or a **sail**?

3. I shine down from the sky. Am I the **son** or the **sun**?

4. I come after three but before five. Am I **four** or **for**?

5. I am a bug and I make honey. Am I a **bee** or a **be**?

Match Time

Match each picture on the left to a picture on the right using two different colored markers or crayons.

Use one color to draw a line between pictures for words that are spelled the same but mean different things.

Use the other color to draw a line between pictures for words that sound alike but are not spelled the same.

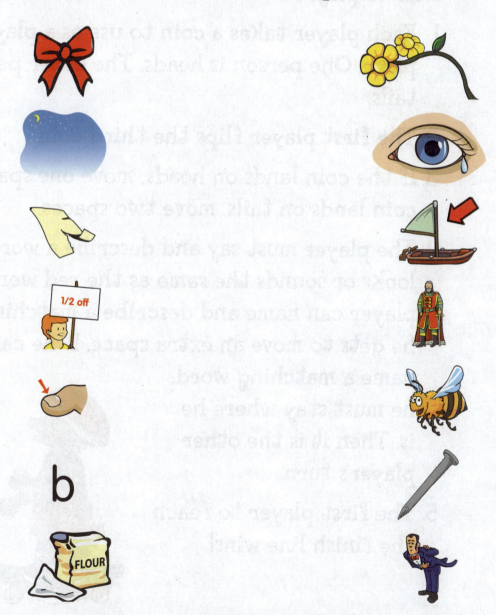

MEGA GAME

Get on Board

Help Slam and Dunk get to the skateboard park.

This is a game for two players.

You will need:
three coins

How to play:

1. Each player takes a coin to use as a playing piece. One person is heads. The other person is tails.

2. The first player flips the third coin.

3. If the coin lands on heads, move one space. If the coin lands on tails, move two spaces.

4. The player must say and describe a word that looks or sounds the same as the red word. If the player can name and describe a matching word, he gets to move an extra space. If he cannot name a matching word, he must stay where he is. Then it is the other player's turn.

5. The first player to reach the finish line wins!

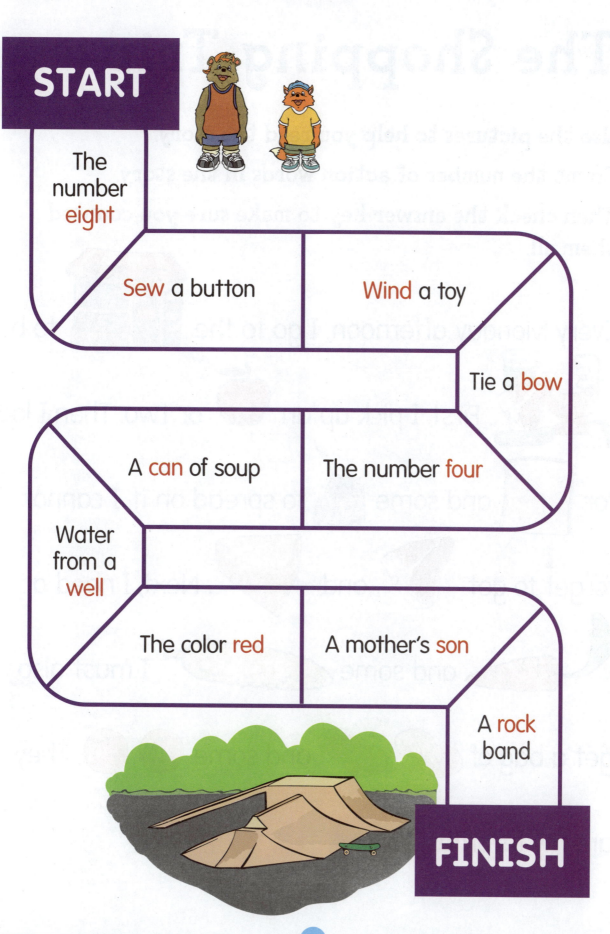

The Shopping Trip

Use the pictures to help you read the story.

Count the number of action words in the story.

Then check the answer Key to make sure you counted them all.

Every Monday afternoon, I go to the to buy . First, I pick up an or two. Then I look for  and some to spread on it. I cannot forget to get and . Next, I need a  and some . I must also get a bag of and some . They are my favorites.

Now count all of the words that are things in the rest of the story.

Then check the answer key to make sure you found them all.

I think that is all the food I need. I take everything up to the cashier and pay for it. The puts all the food into . I put all my in a 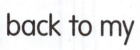. On the way home, I stop at a  to get a slice of pizza. Then I carry all my back to my .

Now I just have to put it all away!

Mystery Pie

Detective Dog has a new case.

Someone baked a blueberry pie and left it outside his door.

He does not know where the pie came from or who baked it.

He wants to thank the person who gave him the pie.

Write down some questions that will help solve the mystery.

Who baked the blueberry pie?

Where _____ ?

Why _____ ?

How _____ ?

What Is the Story?

Draw a line from each question to its matching answer.

Who is driving?   Detective Dog

Why are the cats wet?   They are yelling.

What are the cats doing?   It is raining.

Where are the cats?   They are outside.

All about Me

**Fill in the form below.
It is all about you!**

What is your name? _____

Where do you live? _____

How old are you? _____

What do you like to do? _____

What is your favorite color? _____

What is your favorite sport? _____

What is your favorite animal? _____

_____

Picture Time

Each picture shows one part of a word.
Put the pictures together and guess the whole word.
Find the answer in the word box. Write it on the line.

| bedtime   doorbell   flowerpot   sailboat |

🛏️ + ⏰ = _____

⛵(sail) + 🚣(boat) = _____

🌺 + 🍲 = _____

🚪 + 🔔 = _____

55

The Rainy Day

Read the story.
Some of the pictures show parts of words.
Use the pictures to guess the whole word.
Find the word in the word box and write it on the line.

butterfly   doghouse   pigpen

It was a very rainy day. Detective Dog was rushing to his . He passed by a (🧈 + 🪰) _____ and a sharing an umbrella.

"You two should get out of the rain," he said.

The (🧈 + 🪰) said, "I cannot fly home just yet. My wings will get wet."

The 🐖 said, "My (🐖 + 🖊) _____ is wet from the storm."

Detective Dog told them, "You are welcome to come to my (🐕 + 🏠) _____." So they followed him to his (🐕 + 🏠).

Detective Dog said, "Come in and have some hot chocolate." They happily went inside.

Solve the Riddles

Make words by solving each pair of riddles. Find the word in the word box and write it on the line.

| barnyard | butterfly | eyelid | sandbox |

| What do you put on toast? | + | What likes to buzz around? |

_____

| Where on a farm can you find a pile of hay? | + | What do you call the space behind a house? |

_____

| What do you use to build a castle at the beach? | + | What do you sometimes open when you get a gift? |

_____

| What do you use to see? | + | What fits on top of a pot? |

_____

Crazy Crossword

Each picture shows part of a word.
Use the pictures to solve the clues.
Fill in the answers on the puzzle on the next page.

Across:

1. 🌺 + 🍲

3. ✋ + 🛍️

6. 👁️ + 🛸

Down:

2. 🌳 + 🏠

4. 🐷 + 🖊️

5. 🛏️ + ⏰

Family Fun

Drawing Time

Draw two pictures in each box to make a word from the word box. Each picture should show half of the word.

Put a plus sign between the pictures.

Ask a family member to guess the words you drew.

> jellyfish   keyboard   sandbox
> moonlight   ladybug   raincoat

Note to Parents
Have your child think of words he can make with two other words, and then help him make a scrapbook that shows his words in the form of pictures. You can draw pictures or clip images from newspapers and magazines. When the scrapbook is complete, sound out each of the words.

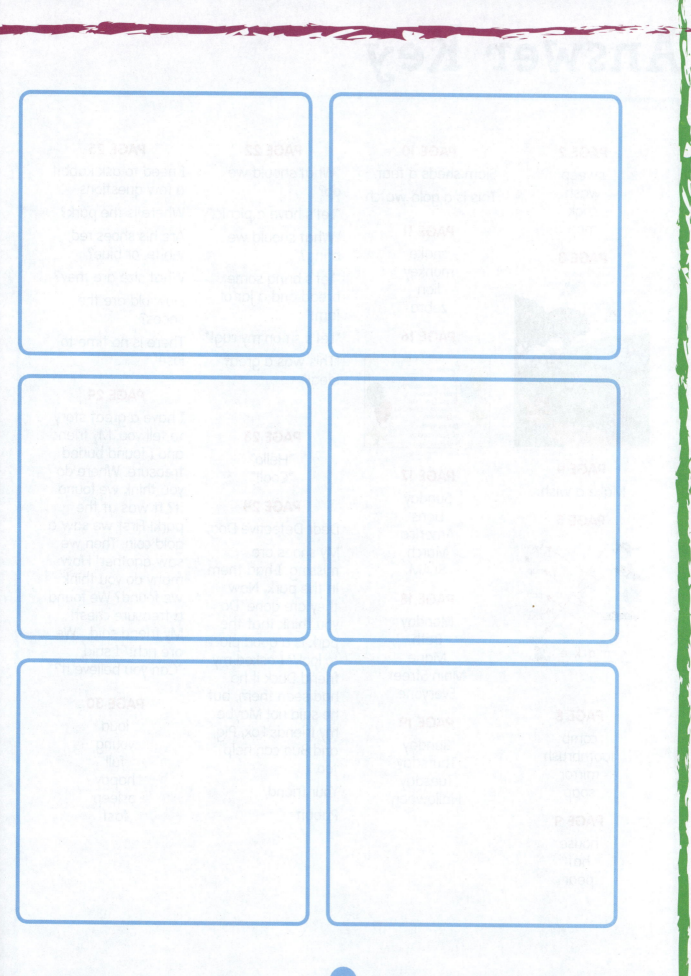

Answer Key

PAGE 2
sweep
wash
cook
mop

PAGE 3

PAGE 4
Make a wish.

PAGE 5

PAGE 8
comb
toothbrush
mirror
soap

PAGE 9
house
hat
pear

PAGE 10
Slam sheds a tear.
This is a gold watch.

PAGE 11
snake
monkey
lion
zebra

PAGE 16

PAGE 17
Sunday
Lions
America
March
SLAM

PAGE 18
Monday
Beth
Marie
Main Street
Everyone

PAGE 19
Sunday
Thursday
Tuesday
Halloween

PAGE 22
"What should we do?"
"Let's have a picnic."
"What should we bring?"
"Let's bring some bread and a jar of jam!"
"Let's sit on my rug!"
"This was a great idea!"

PAGE 23
"Hello"
"Cool!"

PAGE 24
Dear Detective Dog,

My shoes are missing. I had them in the park. Now they are gone. Do you think that the park is a good place to look? I asked my friend Duck if he had seen them, but he said no! Maybe my friends Fox, Pig, and Bug can help too.

Your friend,
Rabbit

PAGE 25
I need to ask Rabbit a few questions.

Where is the park?

Are his shoes red, white, or blue?

What size are they?

How old are the shoes?

There is no time to lose!

PAGE 29
I have a great story to tell you. My friend and I found buried treasure. Where do you think we found it? It was at the park! First we saw a gold coin. Then we saw another! How many do you think we found? We found a treasure chest! My friend said, "We are rich!" I said, "Can you believe it?"

PAGE 30
loud
young
full
happy
asleep
fast

PAGE 31

over — above
messy — dirty
father — dad
storm — rain
simple — easy
little — small
nap — sleep

address

PAGE 32

Across:
1. sick
3. under
6. neat

Down:
2. quick
4. down
5. far

PAGE 33

quick → messy
clean → sad
glad → slow
noisy → quiet

PAGE 34

sad
good

PAGE 35

tall
dry
under
open

PAGE 38

play
rock
bark
play
bark
rock

PAGE 39

pen
saw
wave
note

PAGE 40

tear
note
star
nail
wind

PAGE 41

wind
watch
tear

PAGE 44

heel
He'll
heel
heal
he'll

PAGE 45

be
meet
too

PAGE 46

nose
sail
sun
four
bee

PAGE 47

PAGE 52

answers may vary

PAGE 53

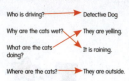

Who is driving? → Detective Dog
Why are the cats wet? → They are yelling.
What are the cats doing? → It is raining.
Where are the cats? → They are outside.

PAGE 55

bedtime
sailboat
flowerpot
doorbell

PAGE 56

butterfly
pigpen
doghouse

PAGE 57

butterfly
barnyard
sandbox
eyelid

PAGE 59

Across:
1. flowerpot
3. handbag
6. eyelid

Down:
2. treehouse
4. pigpen
5. bedtime

I did it!

Congratulations!

_____

has successfully completed this workbook.

2nd Grade
Hooked on Phonics®
Reading Comprehension

Copyright © 2007 Educate Products, LLC. All rights reserved.
Printed in China. No part of this publication may be reproduced, stored in any retrieval system or transmitted, in any form or by any means, electronic, mechanical, photocopying, recording, or otherwise, without the prior written permission of the publisher.

Play It Cool!

Slam and Dunk are hot.

What will cool them down?

Circle the things that will help them cool down.

Draw an X on the things that will not cool them down.

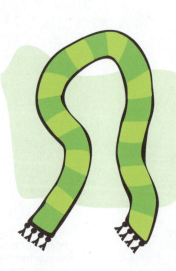

Party On!

You're invited to Dunk's birthday party!
Read your invitation.
Then answer the questions.

1. What time is the party? _____

2. Where is it? _____

3. What is the date of the party? _____

4. What else could you bring to the party?
   (Clue: It has a bow.)
   _____

Cross That Line!

Detective Dog and the runners are heading for the finish line. Look at the picture. Then answer the questions.

1. Who do you think will win? _____

2. What if the leader trips and falls? Who will win then? _____

3. Why won't the rabbit win? _____

4. Why might the cat's feet hurt? _____

Finders Sneakers

Help Detective Dog find his missing sneakers. Read the letter. Then complete the sentences.

1. Detective Dog will find his sneakers if he walks to the _____.

2. The sneakers are in a bird's _____.

3. Detective Dog must _____ the tree to get the sneakers.

4. _____ and _____ sent the letter to Detective Dog.

On the Farm

Read Dunk's letter to Slam. Then answer the questions.

Dear Slam,

I'm sorry to hear that you are sick. I missed you on the school trip today. We visited a farm. We had fun! We saw fields of corn and pumpkins. We saw six black cows. We saw a red barn and a yellow cat. We helped make pumpkin pie and cornbread. We fed the cows. We chased the cat under the fence!

Best of all, we took turns riding the farm horse. It loves to eat carrots and apples.

Hurry and get well!

Your friend,
Dunk

1. Why did Slam miss the school trip? _____

_____

2. What foods did Dunk help cook? _____

3. Which animal likes carrots and apples? _____

4. Which animal was Dunk's favorite? _____

Snack Time

Slam and Dunk want a snack. Look at the sentences. Then draw a line from the sentence to the food that it describes.

I am round, warm, and topped with cheese.

I am a fruit that can be yellow, green, or red.

You can eat me at picnics and ball games.

Monkeys like to gobble me up.

I am small, sweet, and a treat for one person.

Say What?

Draw a line from the sentences in each bubble to the correct animal on the next page. Pretend to be the animal and say the sentences out loud.

- I live in the ocean. I have a long nose. I am gentle and playful.

- I live in the hot plains and forest. I have a long trunk and two long teeth. I am tall and strong.

- I live in warm places. I have many colors. I have a curved beak.

- I live in the ocean. I have many teeth. My tail points up like a fin.

- I live in cold places. I leap and dive in the ocean for fish. I have a black coat and a white bib.

- I live in cold forests. I am covered with warm fur. I sleep during the winter.

- I live in warm forests. I walk with my hands and feet. I have dark fur and I like bananas.

- I live on a farm. I like mud. I squeal and grunt.

Just the Facts!

Invite family members to do this activity with you. Look through magazines and cut out favorite stories. Read the stories out loud. Players ask readers, Why, What If, and How questions about their stories. Then players write down the important details from each story on a piece of paper like the one on the next page.

Take turns retelling the stories from the details. Decide whose stories are closest to the originals.

Note to Parents
This activity will help your child practice gathering, clarifying, and organizing information.

What a Day!

Look at the calendar for October. Answer the questions.

SUNDAY	MONDAY	TUESDAY	WEDNESDAY	THURSDAY	FRIDAY	SATURDAY
1	2	3	4	5	6 🌺	7
8	9	10	11 🪲	12	13	14
15 🎺	16	17	18	19	20	21
22	23	24	25	26	27	28 🐟
29	30	31 🍬				

1. Which date smells the sweetest? _____

2. Which date sounds the loudest? _____

3. Which date feels the wettest? _____

4. Which date looks the softest? _____

What's in the Box?

Slam and Dunk asked their friends to guess what's inside this box. Look at the graph to see how many friends picked each choice. Then answer the questions.

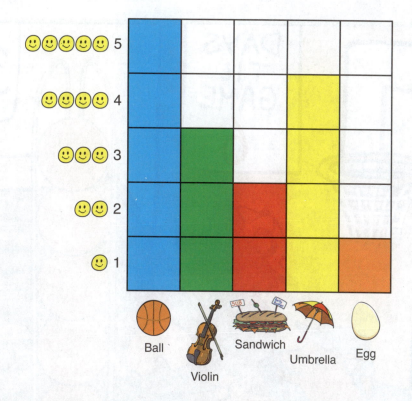

How many friends think a violin is in the box? _____

How many friends think something to eat is in the box? _____

Do more friends think an egg or a violin is in the box? _____

Which choice do most friends think is in the box? _____

Ready to Slam and Dunk!

Slam and Dunk are ready to play basketball. Look at the picture. Circle the sign that shows how many days until the next game.
Draw a rectangle around where the balls are kept.
Draw an X on the basketball hoop.

Busy Bones

This dog loves to hide bones. She has been hiding her bones every day. Look at the stacks of bones. Then answer the questions.

1. How many bones did the dog hide on Saturday? _____

2. On which day did the dog hide the most bones? _____

3. Did the dog hide more bones on Tuesday or on Friday? _____

4. Which day did the dog hide the fewest bones? _____

Slam's Messy Room

Slam and Dunk are cleaning Slam's room. Look at the picture. Then read the sentences. Circle True or False after each sentence.

1. Slam's pillow is on the floor.
   True   False

2. Slam and Dunk are playing ball.
   True   False

3. Slam needs to clean up his room.
   True   False

4. Slam is lying on the bed.
   True   False

Let It Rain!

Detective Dog wrote down the number of days it rained during some months in the spring and summer. Use his chart to answer the questions below.

Month	Number of Rainy Days
April	20
May	13
June	5
July	5
August	0

1. Which month had the most days of rain?

   _____

2. Which month had no rain at all?

   _____

3. Which two months had the same number of rainy days?

   _____

MEGA GAME

A Room of My Own

Try this with a friend. Have you ever dreamed about a perfect room of your own? Draw a picture of the room. Label all of its parts. Then make a list of the special things you put in your room. Tell why you chose each item.

Our Dream Room

What Is in Our Dream Room?

_____

_____

_____

_____

_____

_____

_____

_____

_____

Favorite Things

Choose three people and write their initials on the lines above the top row of the chart.

Then ask them to think of their favorite color, food, animal, and season.

Write or draw their answers in the boxes under their initials.

Now fill in your answers to the questions.

Show the chart to your friends and family. Did any of the people give the same answers?

Note to Parents
Making a chart helps your child organize information and understand what he reads or learns. You can ask your child to make charts about the number of books he reads every month or the kinds of toys he has. Making a chart is a challenging activity. Help your child by making your own charts as examples.

Our Favorite Things

___ ___ ___ ___ Me

Favorite Color				
Favorite Animal				
Favorite Food				
Favorite Season				

Find That Book!

Detective Dog wants to learn about bugs. Circle the books he should read. Draw an X over books that will not help.

Planets in Space

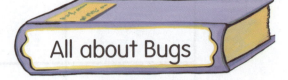
All about Bugs

Let's Visit China!

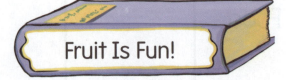
Fruit Is Fun!

Ants Are My Friends

The Queen Bee

By the Book

Detective Dog found a good book. Now he needs to find the answers to his questions. Read the questions below. Then write the number of the chapter where he can find the answer.

Contents

Chapter 1
Beetles, Beetles, Beetles

Chapter 2
Butterflies around the World

Chapter 3
The Buzz on Bees and Flowers

Chapter 4
Hop with Grasshoppers

Chapter 5
Ants and More Ants

1. Where do most butterflies live? _____

2. How many kinds of beetles are there? _____

3. What flowers do bees like best? _____

4. How far can grasshoppers hop? _____

Picture Hunt

Slam and Dunk found some great books in the library. Read each title. Then look at pictures from inside each book. Draw a line from the book title to the pictures from that book.

Snowmen Love Snow

Puppies Are the Best Pets!

Birthday Surprise

The Toy Airplane

Slam and Dunk Snack and Play

Pick a Title

Look at the book covers. Underline the best title for each book.

The Bunny and the Cat

Detective Dog and His Friends

Detective Dog Hears a Noise

Detective Dog's New Home

Detective Dog Hits a High Note

Music around the World

A Starfish on the Sand

Detective Dog's Beach Day

Slam's Story

Read Slam's story. Then write a title for each of the chapters on the lines in the book. Draw pictures for the story on the next page.

Chapter 1 _____

Slam was a tiny cub when he came home with his mother and father for the first time. He could not feed himself. He could not run, jump, or play. He spent most of his time taking a nap in his crib or in his mother's arms. He also cried a lot because he could not talk.

Chapter 2 _____

Slam grew into a bigger cub. He learned to feed himself. He learned to run, jump, and play with friends. He took only one short nap a day. He learned to talk. One day, he climbed on a bus and went to school.

Chapter 3 _____

Now Slam is an even bigger cub. His favorite foods are pizza and ice cream. He likes to play basketball with his best friend Dunk. He doesn't need naps. He rides a bike to school. Slam thinks back to when he was a tiny cub. It seems like a long time ago!

Book Scavenger Hunt

Invite your family on a book scavenger hunt around your home or in a library. Players must find a book about each of the things listed in the first column of the chart. Each player must answer questions about the books he finds. The first player who finishes his list wins the scavenger hunt. Happy hunting!

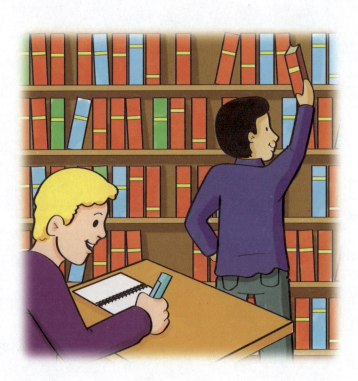

Note to Parents
This activity gives children the opportunity to practice research skills. It is also a great way to familiarize them with the books in your home or in your local library. Encourage your child to add to the list of subjects he wants to learn about.

📖	❓	Answers
Dinosaurs	Does this book have pictures?	_____
Animals	How many pages are in this book?	_____
Planets	What is the title of this booK?	_____
Holidays	Who wrote this book?	_____

What's It All About?

Look at the pictures below. Circle the sentence that tells the main idea of each picture.

Dunk likes building block towers.

Dunk is wearing a yellow shirt.

The chef flips a pizza in the air.

The chef wears a hat.

Slam wears sneakers.

Slam eats ice cream on a hot day.

Detective Dog feeds the ducks.

Detective Dog wears a coat.

The Big Idea

Circle the sentence that tells the main idea of this picture.

This is a chocolate chip cookie.

The ants went home.

Detective Dog looked at the crumbs.

Detective Dog found the cookie thieves!

The ants left crumbs behind.

Details, Details, Details!

Look at the picture below. Write down three more details from the picture. Use the example for help.

The tree's leaves are green.

That's a Sandwich!

Look at the picture. Read the sentences. Circle the main idea. Underline the details.

There is cheese on the sandwich.

The sandwich has four tomato slices on it.

Detective Dog finds a big sandwich.

The sandwich is near the stove.

Main Idea Match-Up

Look at the pictures. Draw a line to match each picture with its main idea.

Slam and Dunk took a bath.

Slam and Dunk fixed their broken airplane.

Dunk told Slam to jump higher.

Slam and Dunk played catch with the basketball.

It's in the Details!

Look at the picture and write a sentence that tells the main idea. Then write down four details from the picture.

Main Idea _____

Detail _____

Detail _____

Detail _____

Detail _____

How Many Details?

Play this game with a friend. Look at the pictures for one minute. Close the book. Then, on a sheet of paper, write down as many details as you can remember from each picture. Count your details. Whoever writes down the most details wins!

Be a Storyteller!

Copy each main idea from the next page onto an index card. Gather your family together and place the cards face down in a pile. Each player reads a card and adds details to make a story. Happy storytelling!

Note to Parents
If your child or anyone else in the family has difficulty crafting a story from start to finish, invite other family members to help create the story by adding details.

My family loves the beach.	I was late for school that day.
My birthday party was the best ever.	My favorite holiday is ___.
Dogs are the best pets.	Dunk has a new baby in his family.

Rain, Rain, Go Away

Read the story. Then answer the questions.

Detective Dog went out for a walk. He stopped when he saw some big, gray clouds. "Hmmm," he thought, "it looks like it's going to rain!" Detective Dog ran home to get his umbrella. Sure enough, when Detective Dog left his house again, it started to rain. Detective Dog's red umbrella kept him dry for the rest of his walk.

1. Why did Detective Dog stop walking?

_____

_____

2. Why did Detective Dog run home?

_____

_____

3. Why didn't Detective Dog get wet?

_____

_____

Hello Duckling!

Read the story. Then answer the questions.

Ducks lay eggs. A duckling grows inside of a duck egg until the duckling is big enough to hatch. Then it makes a crack in the eggshell. It chips through the eggshell and wiggles out. The baby duckling dries itself until it is fluffy. It begins to quack.

1. What happens first when a duckling is big enough to hatch?

_____

_____

2. What happens next?

_____

_____

3. What two things happen after the duckling hatches?

_____

_____

What Will Happen?

Look at each picture. Then read the sentences. Circle the sentence that tells what will probably happen next.

The ice cream will drip on Slam's sneaker.

Dunk will ask for a taste of Slam's ice cream.

Dunk will look for his basketball.

Dunk will play basketball.

Slam and Dunk will start dancing.

Slam and Dunk will go skateboarding.

Dunk will put his sock away.

Dunk will put on his shoe.

Why?

Look at each picture. Then read the sentences. Circle the sentence that tells what probably happened.

The ant bit the carrot. Why?
The ant was hungry.
The ant was thirsty.
The ant was happy.

The cat is scared. Why?
The cat saw a mouse.
The cat saw some food.
The cat saw a big dog.

The mouse is very big. Why?
The mouse is always hungry.
The mouse ate too much cheese.
The mouse lost ten pounds.

The monkey is mad. Why?
Someone gave the monkey a treat.
Someone gave the monkey a present.
Someone ate the monkey's bananas.

Which Goes First?

Draw a line from what Detective Dog says to the correct picture. Then write the numbers 1 through 5 in the boxes to put the pictures in order.

"Then I will search low."

"What is that noise?"

"Ah, I love sitting down with a good book!"

"Of course! It is a puppy playing drums!"

"First, I will search high."

Tell the Tale

These pictures tell a story. Write 1, 2, and 3 in the boxes to show what happened first, next, and last. Then write a sentence on the lines to tell what happened in each picture.

Sing a Story

Play this game with a friend. Look at the beginning of these songs. It is up to you to make up the middle and end. Choose a beginning line. Make up a tune and sing the line. Challenge your friend to continue the song.

Oh, I love to go a-camping!

One day my sneakers walked away.

The hamster has a secret.

Family Fun

If I...

Play this game with your family. Think of the first part of an "If I . . . , then . . ." sentence. Invite family members to think of the rest. For example, "If I had a robot, then it could do my homework while I played outside."

The sillier the idea, the better! Use the lines on the next page to write down your ideas.

More than one family member can respond to the same situation. It is fun to see the different answers that can come from the same beginning!

Note to Parents
This is a fun way for children to explore the concept of cause and effect.

If I _____,

then _____.

If I _____,

then _____.

If I _____,

then _____.

If I _____,

then _____.

If I _____,

then _____.

A Buggy Picnic

Read the story. Answer the questions on the next page.

It was a beautiful day. The sun was shining. The birds were singing. Slam and Dunk decided to have a picnic in the park. Slam brought bananas, cherries, and cheese. Dunk brought sandwiches, peaches, and milk. They set their blanket on the ground under a big tree.

Suddenly, Slam saw a sandwich walking across the grass. "That sandwich is walking!" shouted Slam.

Dunk picked up the sandwich. "The sandwich isn't walking, Slam," said Dunk. "These ants are carrying it away."

Slam and Dunk continued to eat. Suddenly, Dunk jumped up. "I hear buzzing!"

"Bees!" shouted Slam, as he ran around the park.

Finally, the bees flew away and Slam and Dunk sat down to enjoy their picnic. "Eeek!" shouted Dunk.

"What is it?" asked Slam.

"A spider, a spider!" shouted Dunk. He jumped away. "Look," said Dunk, "I have some money. Let's go to the pizza place and have a picnic there instead."

"I'm with you!" said Slam.

Read the sentences. Circle "True" or "False" after each sentence.

1. The bees made the sandwich move.   True   False

2. A spider and some ants came to the picnic.   True   False

3. Slam and Dunk left the picnic because it rained.   True   False

4. Slam brought cherries to the picnic.   True   False

Detective Dog Paints

Read the story. Use the pictures to help you.

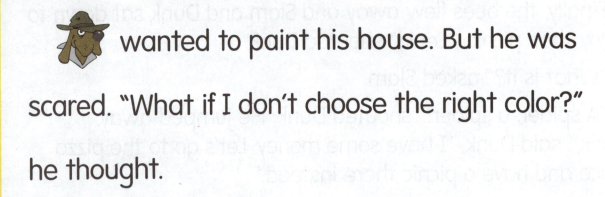

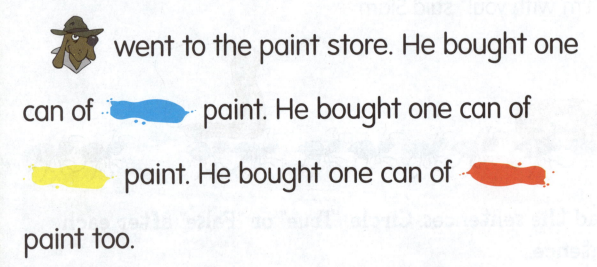

"Now I can try them all!" said .

Next he tried the paint. was . "I don't like the paint," said . "It makes me see ," he said.

Finally, tried the paint. was . "I love the paint!" said . " makes me feel . It is nice and ." finished painting the house .

"It is quite + ny outside," said . "And I'm really + d. It's a perfect day to relax and the paint dry."

That's just what did.

Slam and Dunk Clean

Read the story. Use the pictures to help you.

 and were at home. "I smell something bad," said .

"I think it's the ," said .

"Let's clean the today. We can get a lot done if we work together."

"Okay," said . "Let's work quickly so we can go  + ing later."

 and 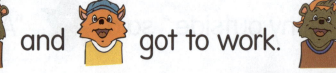 got to work.

+ ped all the floors. + ed all the  went outside and + d all the .

He put them in .  even + ed nails in the wall and hung some pictures. decided to back the curtains to let some light in. Finally they finished.

"Wow!" said . "The place looks great. It makes me want to run and !"

"Not me," said . "The place does look great, but it makes me want to 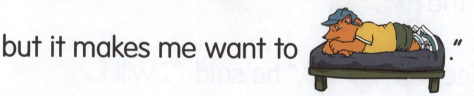."

"Does this mean we are not going to go  + ing?" asked .

There was no answer. was asleep.

Detective Dog's Day

Read the story. Use the pictures to help you.

🕵️ was 🛏️ + ing. Suddenly, he woke up and 🕵️🛏️ + ed.

"What a beautiful day!" he said. "It is very ☀️ + ny. It's a perfect day for the 🏖️!"

🕵️ jumped out of 🛏️ and packed his 🚗. He packed his 🏐. He packed his 🏖️ and a 🥪. 🕵️ left his 🏠 and headed for the 🏖️.

"I will collect 🐚🐚🐚," he said. "I will C ⭐⭐ and maybe even some 🐟🐟. I can't wait to 👂 the 🌊 + s." 🕵️ liked 2 swim in the 〰️, but he hoped he wouldn't C a 🦈!

 got to the . He unpacked his . He unpacked his . He unpacked his  and sat down.

"Ahh," he said, "I am so 🙂." Suddenly, heard something. It sounded like thunder. looked at the sky. He saw many ☁ ☁. Then he felt some 💧.

"Oh, no!" said . "It's raining!"

 ran to his .

"I packed my . I packed my and my ," he said. "But I sure am glad I remembered to pack my !"

Picture Stories

Play this game with a friend. Make your own story using the pictures on this page. Use the lines on the next page to write. Copy the pictures into your story. Take turns reading your stories to each other.

Picture Story

Gather magazines and cut out pictures for a picture story. Think about what kind of story you might want to tell. These questions will help you begin:

Where does my story take place?

Who are the characters in my story?

What might happen in my story?

How will my story end?

You can work together as a family on one picture story or you can each work on your own story. Use the lines on the next page to write your picture story. You can paste your pictures on the page. Have fun sharing your stories!

Note to Parents
This activity will reinforce your child's understanding of the elements of a story. Help him to ask and answer the key questions—how, what, when, where, who, and why—as he shapes his story.

Answer Key

PAGE 66
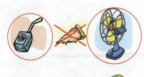

PAGE 67
1. 2:30-4:30 p.m.
2. Skateboard Park
3. Saturday, June 28
4. a present

PAGE 68
1. the mouse
2. Detective Dog
3. The rabbit is sleeping.
4. The boots might hurt its feet.

PAGE 69
1. park
2. nest
3. climb
4. Slam; Dunk

PAGE 70
1. He was sick.
2. pumpkin pie; cornbread
3. the farm horse
4. the farm horse

PAGE 71

PAGES 72–73

PAGE 76
1. October 6
2. October 15
3. October 28
4. October 31

PAGE 77
three
three
violin
ball

PAGE 78

PAGE 79
1. two
2. Sunday
3. Tuesday
4. Thursday

PAGE 80
1. True
2. True
3. True
4. False

PAGE 81
1. April
2. August
3. June; July

PAGE 86

PAGE 87
1. Chapter 2
2. Chapter 1
3. Chapter 3
4. Chapter 4

PAGE 88

PAGE 89

PAGE 90
Possible titles:

Chapter 1: Baby Slam

Chapter 2: School Days

Chapter 3: Big Slam

PAGE 94

PAGE 95
Detective Dog found the cookie thieves!

PAGE 96
Possible details:

The mother feeds the baby birds.

The grass is green.

The sky is blue.

Detective Dog wears a gray coat.

PAGE 97

PAGE 98

Slam and Dunk took a bath.

Slam and Dunk fixed their broken airplane.

Dunk told Slam to jump higher.

Slam and Dunk played catch with the basketball.

PAGE 99

Possible answers:

Main Idea: Detective Dog loves to play with the kittens.

Detail: Detective Dog holds one kitten.

Detail: There are three kittens in the basket.

Detail: There is a ball of yarn by Detective Dog's foot.

Detail: Two of the kittens are brown.

PAGE 104

1. Detective Dog saw big, gray clouds. He thought it looked like rain.
2. Detective Dog ran home to get his umbrella.
3. Detective Dog's umbrella kept him dry.

PAGE 105

1. The duckling makes a crack in the eggshell.
2. The duckling chips through the eggshell and wiggles out.
3. The duckling dries itself until it is fluffy. It begins to quack.

PAGE 106

The ice cream will drip on Slam's sneaker.
Dunk will ask for a taste of Slam's ice cream.

Dunk will look for his basketball.
Dunk will play basketball.

Slam and Dunk will start dancing.
Slam and Dunk will go skateboarding.

Dunk will put his sock away.
Dunk will put on his shoe.

PAGE 107

The ant bit the carrot. Why?
The ant was hungry.
The ant was thirsty.
The ant was happy.

The cat is scared. Why?
The cat saw a mouse.
The cat saw some food.
The cat saw a big dog.

The mouse is very big. Why?
The mouse is always hungry.
The mouse ate too much cheese.
The mouse lost ten pounds.

The monkey is mad. Why?
Someone gave the monkey a treat.
Someone gave the monkey a present.
Someone ate the monkey's bananas.

PAGE 108

"Then I will search low." — 5
"What is that noise?" — 1
"Ah, I love sitting down with a good book!" — 3
"Of course! It is a puppy playing drums!" — 2
"First, I will search high." — 4

PAGE 109

 3 Possible sentences: Slam and Dunk fixed the broken plane.

 2 Slam climbed the tree to get the broken plane.

 1 Slam and Dunk played with a remote-controlled plane.

PAGE 115

1. False
2. True
3. False
4. True

I did it!

Congratulations!

_____

has successfully completed this workbook.

2nd Grade
Hooked on Phonics®
Spelling

Copyright © 2007 Educate Products, LLC. All rights reserved.
Printed in China. No part of this publication may be reproduced, stored in any retrieval system or transmitted, in any form or by any means, electronic, mechanical, photocopying, recording, or otherwise, without the prior written permission of the publisher.

c or k?

Write a "c" or "k" to complete each word.

__at   __iss   __ake

__ing   __ite   __ap

c or s?

Write a "c" or "s" to complete each word.
Draw lines to match each word to a picture.

| __ix | __ity | __alt |

| __ents | __ock | __un |

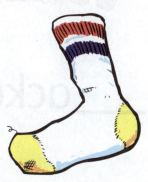

g or j?

Write a "g" or "j" to complete each word.

___ellyfish ___et ___em

___acket ___ym ___am

Golly g

Circle all the words that begin with the g sound as in go.

gate   gem   gym

giant   goat   gum

b, bl, or br?

Write the letter or letters that begin each word. Then draw a line from each picture to the letter or letters that complete the word.

__ow   __aby   __us

b   bl   br

__oom   __ick   __ue

Which Bone?

I did it!

Help Mad Dog make some words.
Color the bone that completes each word.

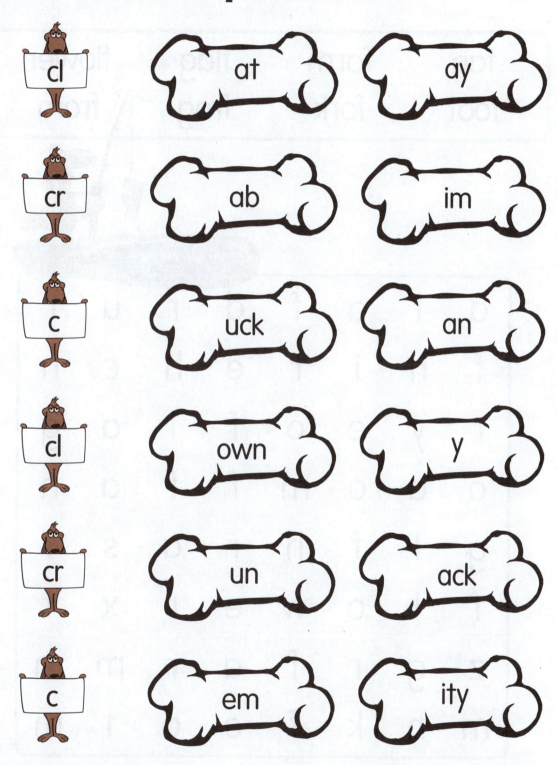

Word Hunt

Circle each word you find in the puzzle. Look across and down.

fan   farm   flag   flower
foot   fork   frog   from

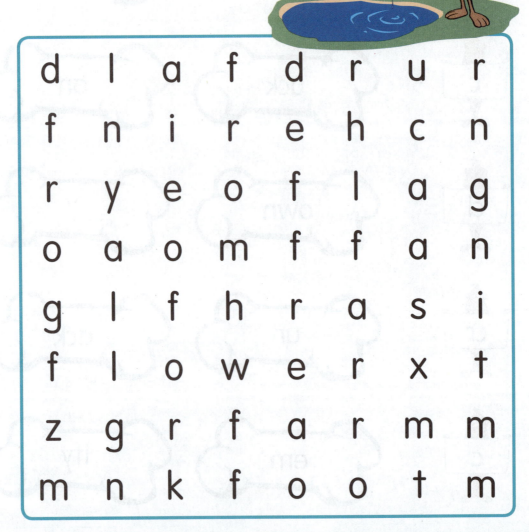

```
d l a f d r u r
f n i r e h c n
r y e o f l a g
o a o m f f a n
g l f h r a s i
f l o w e r x t
z g r f a r m m
m n k f o o t m
```

Play Practice

The Ratinis are putting on a play. Help them find the props they need. Circle the things in each row that begin with the letters they are looking for.

Swell Starts

Draw a line from each picture and word beginning to the letters that complete the word.

sled	sl	ar
spill	sp	arf
star	st	ow
snow	sn	ed
swan	sw	irt
skirt	sk	an
scarf	sc	ill

Bright Beginnings

Look at each picture.
Write the missing letters that complete each word.

| br | cr | dr | fr | pr | tr |

__ead   __um   __own

__og   __uck   __ince

s, ss, or zz?

Write the ending letters "s," "ss," or "zz" to finish the words in each sentence.

Mad Dog ha____ a gla____ of milk.

Bees bu____ around a flower.

Mad Dog knocks over hi____ gla____.

Now the bees bu____ around the milk.

ff or ll?

Write the ending letters "ff" or "ll" to finish the words in each sentence. Then match the sentences to the pictures.

Look at Mad Dog hu____ and pu____.

Cat wi____ hit the ba____ over the wa____.

Last Letters

Help Cat wash the dishes.
Color the bubble that completes each word.

si   (nk) (nt)
si   (nd) (ng)
bu   (mp) (nd)
ra   (st) (ft)
sa   (lt) (mp)
te   (lf) (nt)
ve   (nk) (st)
bri (lt) (ng)
e   (ft) (lf)

Same Sound

Say each picture name out loud. Fill in the missing letters to finish the word that rhymes with it.

| ft | lt | lf | mp | nd | ng | nk | nt | st |

du__

ri__

ne__

se__

la__

ri__

me__

she__

li__

Same Letters

This is a game for two or more players.

You will need:
one coin

How to play:

1. The first player flips a coin. If it lands on heads, say a word that has the same beginning letter or letters as a word in the Heads box on the next page. If it lands on tails, say a word with the same ending letter or letters as a word in the Tails box on the next page. Each time you use a word in the Heads or Tails box, cross it out.

2. The second player flips a coin. He says a word with either the same beginning letters as a word in the Heads box or the same ending letters as a word in the Tails box.

3. The players take turns until all the words in the Heads and Tails boxes have been used.

Heads

game	stop	drip
play	from	city

Tails

sand	doll	think
was	soft	jump

Scavenger Hunt

This game is for two or more players.

How to play:

1. Using the chart on the next page, one player calls out beginning or ending letters.

2. Both players try to think of something that begins or ends with those letters. The first player to think of a word that begins or ends with those letters gets a point. Then the player who gets the point calls out the next letters.

3. The first player to get ten points wins!

Note to Parents
This activity helps your child become more familiar with beginning and ending blends. If he has trouble thinking of words with these beginning and ending blends, give him clues until he guesses the word.

Beginnings	Endings
c____	____ft
g____	____ll
bl____	____lt
cl____	____mp
cr____	____nd
fl____	____ng
fr____	____nk
pl____	____nt
st____	____ss
tr____	____st

Rhyme Time

Draw a line from each word on the left to the word on the right that rhymes with it.

man	leg
hit	rub
sock	can
egg	fit
tub	frog
camp	hen
men	clock
log	lamp

Dig It

Write the word that completes each sentence. Use the word box to help you.

> dig   get   hot   map   sun

Mad Dog and Cat have a _____.

Cat and Mad Dog _____ in the boat.

The _____ made Cat and Mad Dog _____.

Now Mad Dog can _____ for gold!

Crazy a

Add an "e" to the end of each word to make the long a sound.

Then draw a line from the new word to its matching picture.

tap__

cap__

man__

can__

plan__

i Time

Unscramble the word that goes with each picture. Write the word on the line.

edim
_____

irp
_____

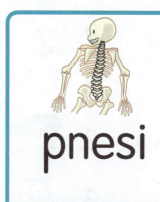
pnesi
_____

rife
_____

teki
_____

inf
_____

O No!

Use the picture clues and the word box to fill in the puzzle.

| stop | mop | hop |
| stove | note | phone |

Across: 1. 🐰
4. 🍳
5. 🧹

Down: 2. ☎️
3. 📝
4.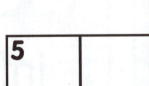

Tub Fun

Circle each word you find in the puzzle.
Look across and down.

clue	cube	cute
huge	mule	tube

t u b e x b c
n d s h a p l
e o c u b e u
a q o g s g e
c u t e y e s
j f m u l e l

ch or sh?

Help Cat pick the flowers.
Color the flower that completes each word.

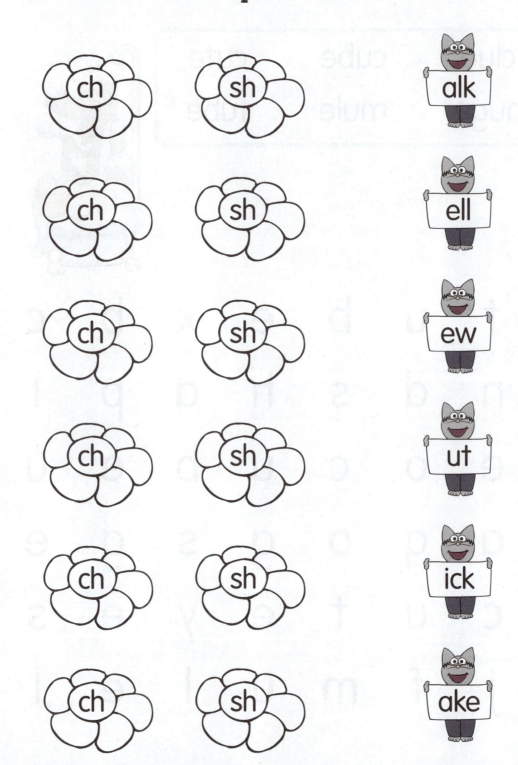

sh or th?

Help the Ratini take a bath.
Color the bubble that begins each word.

sh	th	ip
sh	th	ose
sh	th	op
sh	th	em
sh	th	ut
sh	th	is
sh	th	ake

Acting Out

This is a game for two or more players.

You will need:
one coin

How to play:

1. The first player flips the coin. If it lands on heads, act out a word in the Heads box on the next page. If it lands on tails, act out a word in the Tails box on the next page. The other players should guess the word.

2. The second player flips the coin. He acts out a different word from the Heads or Tails box.

3. The players take turns until all of the words have been acted out.

4. Play some more with other words you have learned!

Heads

rip	hop	cut
chop	ship	shut

Tails

phone	tape	dive
shake	shine	chase

Tell and Spell

This is a game for two players.

How to play:

1. Copy each word from the list on the next page onto an index card.
2. Shuffle the cards and deal each player nine cards.
3. The first player reads the word on one card out loud.

4. The other player spells the word. If the player spells the word correctly, the first player gives him the card. If the player does not spell the word correctly, the first player keeps the card.
5. Keep taking turns until you have correctly spelled the words on all of the cards. The player with the most cards at the end of the game wins.

Note to Parents
This activity will help your child review high-frequency words and words with short and long vowel sounds. If your child has trouble spelling the words on the list, try focusing on two to three words each week.

cape	note
clock	plane
come	rub
cute	said
dime	says
from	ten
kite	that
leg	was
map	were

Room in the Middle

Look at each picture.

Write "oo" or "ue" to complete each word.

sp___n   m___n   cl___

r___f   bl___   r___m

ai or ay?

I did it!

Write "ai" or "ay" to complete the word in each sentence.

Will you pl___ ___ ball with me?

The r___ ___n made the grass wet.

Black and white make gr___ ___.

I will w___ ___t for you to come over.

Can you st___ ___ and play?

The blue p___ ___nt is still wet.

The n___ ___l is sharp.

The ch___ ___n on my bike broke.

oa or ow?

Look at each picture.
Write "oa" or "ow" to complete the word.

   sn__ __

   g__ __t

   bl__ __

   s__ __p

   t__ __d

   b__ __

ee or ea?

Look at each picture.
Write "ee" or "ea" to complete each word.

wh_ _l   tr_ _   m_ _t

 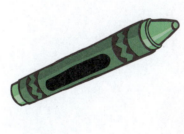 

r_ _d   gr_ _n   b_ _ch

Write a Poem

Help complete the poem. Use the words in the word box to help you. Make sure that each poem rhymes.

day	gray	say
green	mean	seen
blue	clue	true

Listen to what I have to _____,

A color I love is _____,

It is the color of a rainy _____.

This is just what I _____,

A color I love is _____,

It is the color of grass I have _____.

This color is the best, it is _____,

I will give you a _____,

My favorite color of all is _____.

Family Fun

Rhyme Time

This is a game for two players.

You will need:

index cards

How to play:

1. Write each word in the word box on the next page on an index card.

2. Mix up the cards and place them face down on a table in rows.

3. The first player flips over two cards. The player says and spells the words on the cards. If the words rhyme, like moon and spoon, a match has been made. Players keep the matches they make. If the cards do not make a match, the first player should turn them face down again.

4. The second player takes his turn. He tries to find two cards that match.

5. The player who has the most pairs of cards at the end of the game wins.

Note to Parents
This activity encourages children to recognize words with similar vowel sounds. Point out to your child that sometimes the same vowel sound is spelled in different ways. For example, you might say that the words *play* and *rain* have the same long **a** sound, but have different spellings.

boat	broom
chain	day
goat	meal
may	nail
moon	play
rain	room
snail	spoon
stay	wheel

Word Hunt

Look at each picture. Say its name out loud. Then circle the word in the puzzle.

Look across and down.

```
j  a  r  d  e  g
p  h  t  s  d  y
d  e  o  p  l  a
n  a  f  c  g  r
v  r  b  a  r  n
m  t  a  r  m  k
```

ar or or?

I did it!

Draw a line from each picture to the letters that complete each word.

Write the letters on the lines to spell the word.

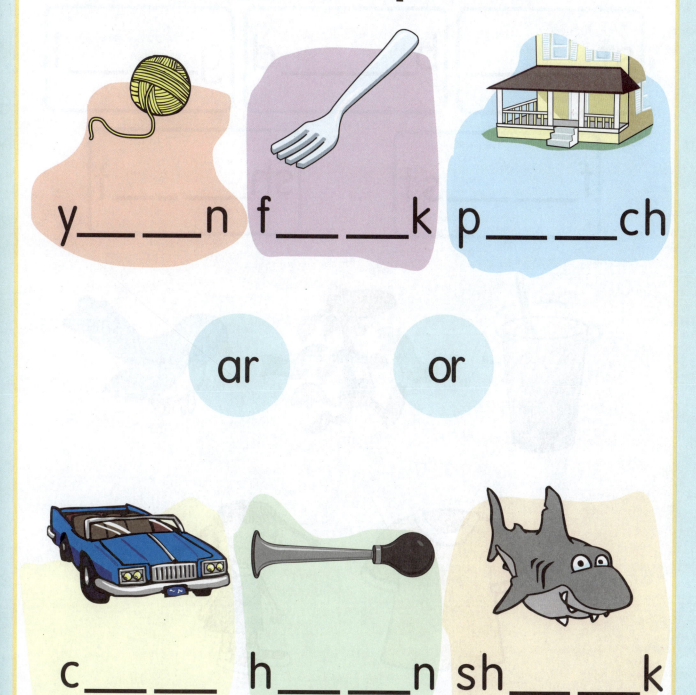

y____n   f____k   p____ch

ar   or

c____   h____n   sh____k

First Place Words

Write the letters "ir" to complete each word.
Then draw a line from the word to its matching picture.

st___   b___d   g___l

f___st   sh___t

It's Your Turn!

Unscramble the word that goes with each picture. Write the word on the line.

 sernu

 lettur

_____ _____

 rucl

 ruf

_____ _____

 trnu

 psure

_____ _____

er, ir, or ur?

Help the Ratini make some more words. Circle the ending that completes each word.

Give It a Try!

I did it!

Write a "y" to complete each word.
Then draw a line from each word to its matching picture.

bab__

fl__

penn__

cr__

pupp__

sk__

MEGA GAME

Concentrate!

You will need:

index cards

How to play:

1. Write each word in the word box on an index card.

2. Mix up the cards and place them face down on a table in rows.

3. The first player flips over two cards. For two cards to match, both words must contain the same vowel. Players keep the matches they make. If they do not have a match, they place both cards face down with the others.

4. The second player takes his turn.

5. The player with the most cards at the end of the game wins.

barn	car
bird	curl
clerk	fur
fork	horn
girl	porch
turn	sport
bark	yard

Family Fun

Make Some Words

This is a game for two players.

You will need:

index cards

crayons

a paper bag

How to play:

1. Make an index card for each of the single letters and each of the two-letter endings on the next page.

2. Place the single-letter cards into a paper bag. Place the two-letter cards face down in a pile.

3. Have the first player pick a single-letter card from the bag and the top card from the two-letter ending pile. See if the cards make a word. If they do, keep the single-letter card and return the two-letter card to the bottom of the pile. If they don't, return the single-letter card to the bag.

4. Take turns picking letters and endings. The player who has the most single-letter cards at the end of the game wins.

> **Note to Parents**
> If your child has trouble thinking of a word that begins with the letter chosen and contains "ar," "or," "ir," or "ur," play a variation of the game by giving some word choices. For example, if your child is trying to make a word that begins with "b" and contains "ar," you could say, "Which word can you make—*barn* or *burn*?

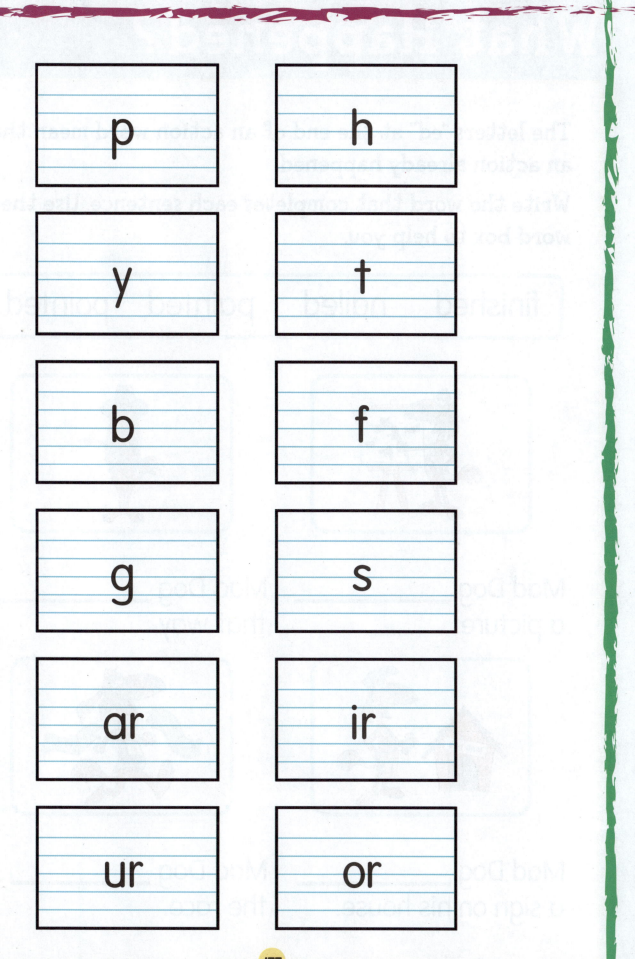

What Happened?

The letters "ed" at the end of an action word mean that an action already happened.

Write the word that completes each sentence. Use the word box to help you.

| finished   nailed   painted   pointed |

Mad Dog _____ a picture.

Mad Dog _____ that way.

Mad Dog _____ a sign on his house.

Mad Dog _____ the race.

Fun with ing!

The letters "ing" at the end of an action word mean that an action is happening now. Choose the word in the word box that describes what each Ratini is doing. Write the word below each picture.

> thinking   climbing   swinging   painting

ed or ing?

Circle "ed" or "ing" to complete the word in each sentence. Then write the letters in the blank space.

I burn____ the toast this morning. ed ing

We are spray_____ the flowers with water. ed ing

The leaf is float_____ down from the tree. ed ing

The candles on the cake are burn____. ed ing

Dad spray____ the pan with olive oil. ed ing

Jen is scoop_____ sand into the pail. ed ing

The balloon float____ up to the ceiling. ed ing

What's Missing?

Write the word that completes each sentence. Use the word box to help you.

| holding | sleeping |
| washed | wished |

Mad Dog _____ his arm.

Cat is _____ a bag.

Cat _____ for a fun gift.

Mad Dog is _____.

Take Two

Make each word plural by taking the letter "y" away and adding the letters "ies."

butterfly   butterflies

candy   cand_____

strawberry   strawberr_____

penny   penn_____

Get Carried Away!

Use the words in the box to write a caption for each picture.

| carried | cried | dried | tried |

The dog _____ a shoe in his mouth.

The monkey _____.

Cat _____ to fix his bike.

The towel _____ in the sun.

Find the Matches!

These words need the letters "es" to make them plural. Write "es" on the line to change each word.

Then draw a line from each word to its matching picture.

fox____ ____

bench____ ____

dish____ ____

bus____ ____

dress____ ____

beach____ ____

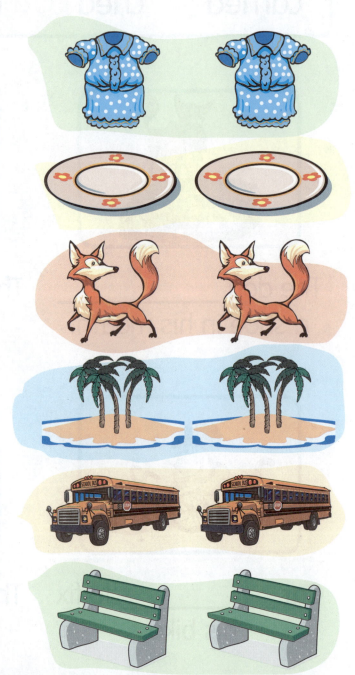

s or es?

Change the ending of each word to make it plural. Write the word on the s box if you add an "s." Write the word on the es box if you add "es."

| bone | cow | ditch | dress |
| inch | nest | stamp | wish |

My Journal

Fill in the journal on this page. Use the word box on the next page for help, or think of your own action words. Then draw a picture of yourself doing one of these things on the next page.

Last week I _____.

Yesterday I _____.

This morning I _____.

Right now I am _____.

Tomorrow I could _____.

Next week I would like to _____.

smile	trying	finished
play	playing	played
rest	resting	rested
read	hugging	danced

Charades!

This is a game for two or more players.

You will need:

index cards

How to play:

1. Write the words in the box on index cards.
2. Turn the cards face down and place them on a table.
3. The first player chooses a card and acts out the word on the card.
4. The other players try to guess the word. They write their answers on a piece of paper like the one shown on the next page.
5. Then the other players show the words that they wrote down. If none of the words is correct, the first player may try acting out the word again.
6. Take turns until all of the cards have been acted out.

Note to Parents
A game of charades is an imagination-building exercise for all members of the family. By acting out various action words, your child deepens his comprehension of what each word means.

climbing frowning jumping kicking
pulling resting singing sleeping
spraying sweeping

1. _____ 6. _____

2. _____ 7. _____

3. _____ 8. _____

4. _____ 9. _____

5. _____ 10. _____

Answer Key

PAGE 130
cat; kiss; cake; king; kite; cap

PAGE 131
S_ix C_ity S_alt
C_ents S_ock S_un
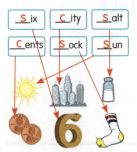

PAGE 132
jellyfish; jet; gem; jacket; gym; jam

PAGE 133

gate gem gym

giant goat gum

PAGE 134
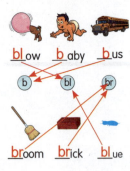
bl_ow b_aby b_us
broom brick blue

PAGE 135
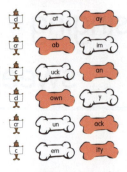

PAGE 136

PAGE 137

PAGE 138
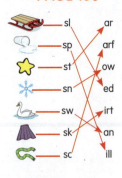
sl — ar
sp — arf
st — ow
sn — ed
sw — irt
sk — an
sc — ill

PAGE 139
bread; drum; crown
frog; truck; prince

PAGE 140
has; glass; buzz;
his; glass; buzz

PAGE 141
Look at Mad Dog
hu_ff and
pu_ff
Cat wi_ll hit the
ba_ll over the
wa_ll

PAGE 142

PAGE 143
dump; ring; nest;
sent; land; rink;
melt; shelf; lift

PAGE 148
man — leg
hit — rub
sock — can
egg — fit
tub — frog
camp — hen
men — clock
log — lamp

PAGE 149
map; get; sun;
hot; dig

PAGE 150
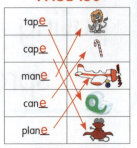

PAGE 151
dime; rip; spine;
fire; kite; fin

PAGE 152
Across:
 1. hop
 4. stove
 5. mop

Down:
 2. phone
 3. note
 4. stop

PAGE 153
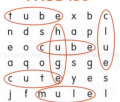

PAGE 154
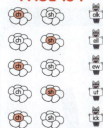

PAGE 155
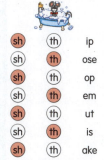

PAGE 160
spoon; moon; clue; roof; blue; room

PAGE 161
play; rain; gray; wait; stay; paint; nail; chain

PAGE 162
snow; goat; blow; soap; toad; bow

PAGE 163
wheel; tree; meat; read; green; beach

PAGE 165
say; gray; day; mean; green; seen; true; clue; blue

PAGE 168
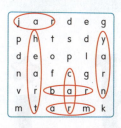

PAGE 169
yarn; fork; porch; car; horn; shark

PAGE 170

PAGE 171
nurse; turtle; curl; fur; turn; purse

PAGE 172

PAGE 173
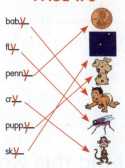

PAGE 178
painted; pointed; nailed; finished

PAGE 179
painting; swinging; climbing; thinking

PAGE 180
burned; spraying; floating; burning; sprayed; scooping; floated

PAGE 181
washed; holding; wished; sleeping

PAGE 182
candies; strawberries; pennies

PAGE 183
carried; cried; tried; dried

PAGE 184
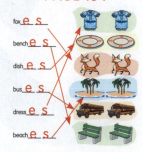

PAGE 185
"s" box: cows, nests, stamps

"es" box: bones, ditches, dresses, inches, wishes

I did it!

Congratulations!

_____

_____

_____

has successfully completed this workbook.

2nd Grade

Hooked on Math®

Addition and Subtraction

Copyright © 2007 Educate Products, LLC. All rights reserved.
Printed in China. No part of this publication may be reproduced, stored in any retrieval system or transmitted, in any form or by any means, electronic, mechanical, photocopying, recording, or otherwise, without the prior written permission of the publisher.

The Number Line

Count the numbers in the number line from 1 to 100.

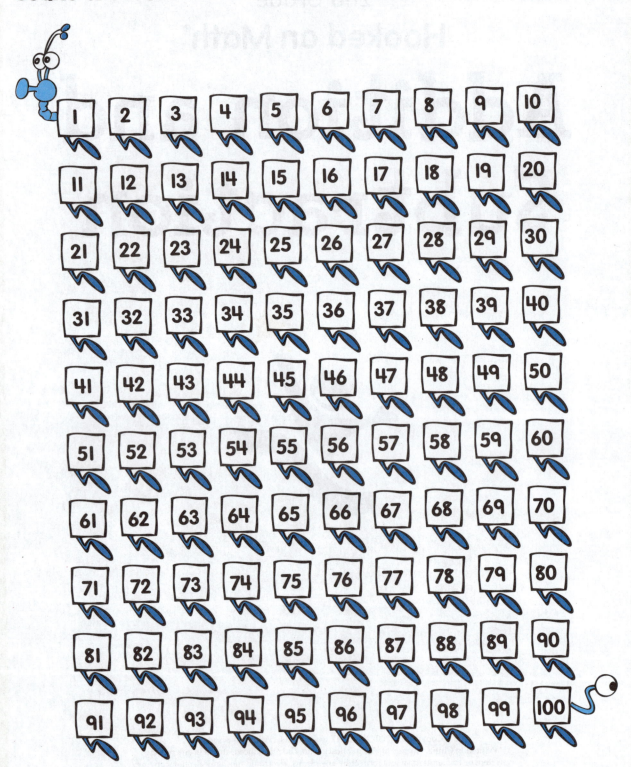

Count by 2s and 5s

Pop Fox wants to show you how to count by 2s. When you count by 2s, you skip over every other number. Try it for yourself!

1	2	3	4	5	6	7	8	9	10
11	12	13	14	15	16	17	18	19	20

Counting by 5s can help you save time. When you count by 5s, you skip over four numbers each time. Look at the numbers below. Every fifth number is colored blue. Practice counting by 5s!

1	2	3	4	5	6	7	8	9	10
11	12	13	14	15	16	17	18	19	20

Add Them Up!

Solve each problem.
Write the sum on the line.

2+1= ___

1+3= ___

4+2= ___

5+1= ___

3+2= ___

4+1= ___

2+4= ___

5+2= ___

4+3= ___

Flower Match

Solve each problem.

Draw a line between the problem and the flower containing its answer. Color the answer flower to match.

In the Bucket!

Throw the balls in the right buckets!

Solve each problem. Write the sum on the line. Then draw a line between each problem and the bucket that shows its answer.

7+3= ____

7+4= ____

5+6= ____

9+3= ____

8+2= ____

4+7= ____

2+10= ____

6+6= ____

8+3= ____

12

11

10

Find the Key

Help the alien find the special Key.

Solve each problem.

Find out which problem adds up to 18. That is the special Key!

Color the special Key yellow.

 _____

 _____

 _____

 _____

 _____

 _____

Take the Cake!

A number sentence is called an equation. Write an equation about each picture. Then solve the problem. For example,

 - ___ = ___

This can be written: 5-1= ___

Now it's your turn. Write the equation for each picture.

___ - ___ = ___

___ - ___ = ___

___ - ___ = ___

Choo! Choo!

Pop Fox can't get the train to start. Solve the problems. Each time you find an answer to a problem, cross out its number on the train car. When you've crossed out all the numbers, the train will start!

10−2= ___ 　　11−2= ___

12−6= ___ 　　6−3= ___

8−8= ___ 　　12−7= ___

Shark!

The shark is hungry! How much food will the shark eat? Write an equation for each of the word problems. Then solve the problems.

1. There are 18 fish. The shark eats 2 of them. How many are left?

    ____ - ____ = ____

2. There are 15 donuts. The shark eats 3 of them. How many are left?

    ____ - ____ = ____

3. There are 17 apples. The shark eats 7 of them. How many are left?

    ____ - ____ = ____

Match the Socks!

Pop Fox needs your help matching his socks. Solve the problems. Find the socks that have the same answer. Then color the matching socks the same color.

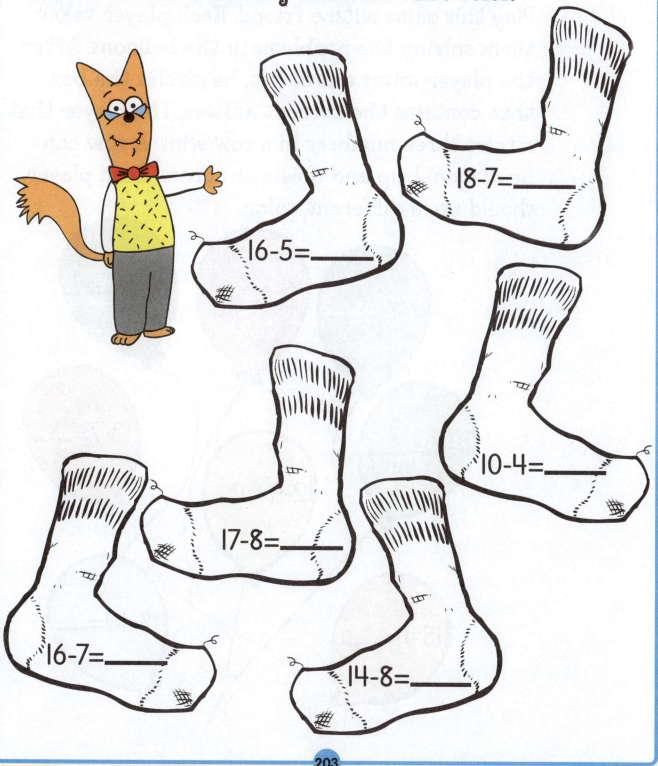

16-5=____

18-7=____

10-4=____

17-8=____

16-7=____

14-8=____

Tic-tac-toe with a Twist

Play this game with a friend. Each player takes turns solving the problems in the balloons. After the player solves a problem, he circles the box that contains the correct answer. The player that circles three numbers in a row wins. A row can be diagonal, up and down, or across. Each player should use a different color.

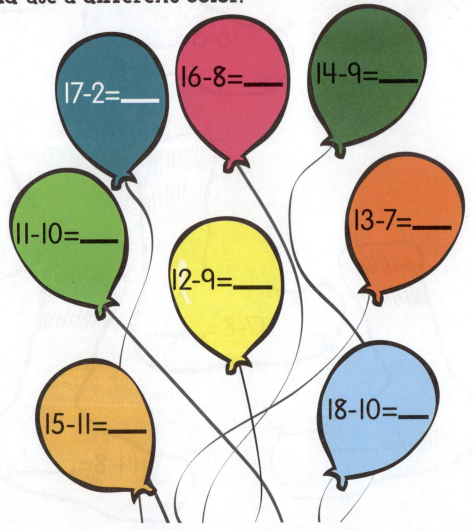

8	6	5
10	9	1
7	4	3

Grocery Store

Play Grocery Store with a friend or family member. Pretend that you run a grocery store and your friends are your customers. Make believe that each person has $15.00 to spend.

Let your customers decide which items they want from the next page. Add up the cost of their purchases and give them change!

Note to Parents
Playing "grocery store" is a great way to mix math with make-believe play. Give your child a chance to figure out the simple addition and subtraction problems in his head. Show patience by allowing him to figure out the answers even if it takes a little time.

soap $2.00

bread $3.00

bubble bath $4.00

milk $2.00

pizza $6.00

apples $2.00

Who's Coming?

The aliens have a lot of friends! Count up all the friends that are coming to their party. Solve each problem. Write the sum on the line.

```
  14          19
 +12         +11
 ___         ___

  15          13
 +10         +12
 ___         ___
```

How Many Hats?

The Ratini Brothers love hats. Read the word problems. Then write equations and solve the problems!

1. One brother has 22 hats. Then another brother gives him 14 hats. How many hats are there in all?

   ____ + ____ = ____

2. One brother has 15 hats. Another brother brings 25 hats. How many hats are there in all?

   ____ + ____ = ____

3. One brother has 33 hats. Another brother has 27 hats. How many hats do they have in all?

   ____ + ____ = ____

Regroup and Add!

Aliens know how to regroup. Do you? If the ones column adds up to a number greater than 9, keep the ones and carry the tens to the tens column. Look at how this is done in the example. Then solve the problems.

```
  1
  ^26
+ 15
─────
  41
```

```
   44         53         55
  +27        +38        +26
  ───        ───        ───


   67         79         84
  +18        +16        +17
  ───        ───        ───
```

Turn on the Light!

Help the alien see the light. Solve the problems below. Then color the light bulbs.

72
+18

59
+12

91
+29

109
+ 5

Alien Match-up

Find a matching pair of aliens.

Add the numbers in that pair on a separate piece of paper.

Point to the answer here.

114   61   113   84   54

28

66

45

99

Now play a different game with a friend or family member.

One player chooses a card.

The other player touches any other card.

Each player must add the two numbers on a separate sheet of paper.

Did you get the same answer?

Helmet Race

The aliens are getting ready to take off.
Help them find their helmets.
Solve each problem.
Draw a line to the correct answer.

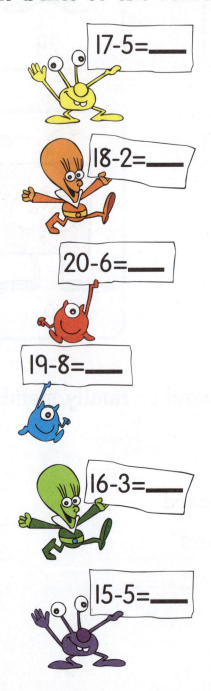

17-5=____

18-2=____

20-6=____

19-8=____

16-3=____

15-5=____

10

13

11

16

12

14

Answer Maze

Take the Ratinis to their friend the clown.
Solve each problem.
Circle the correct answer.
Follow the path with the correct answers through the maze.

1. $20-3=$ ___
2. $18-9=$ ___
3. $14-6=$ ___
4. $12-5=$ ___
5. $13-7=$ ___
6. $17-8=$ ___

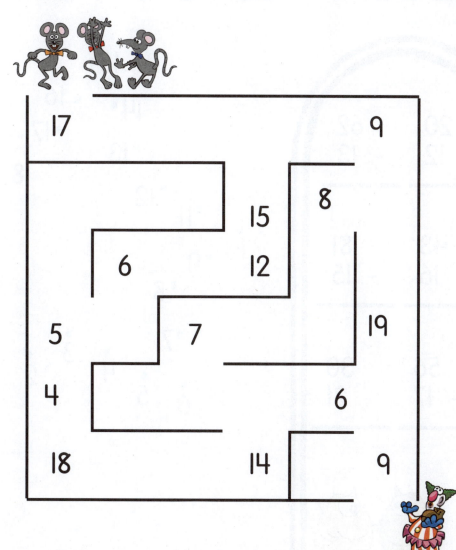

Open the Door!

The aliens need to solve problems to find out what is behind the door.

You can help them.

Solve the problems.

Follow the dots to see what the aliens found behind the door.

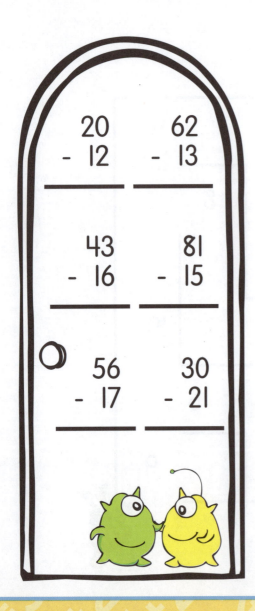

```
  20      62
- 12    - 13
----    ----

  43      81
- 16    - 15
----    ----

  56      30
- 17    - 21
----    ----
```

Balloon Match

The aliens are looking for balloons that match.
You can help them.
Solve each problem.
Find the balloon with the correct answer.
Color those balloons the same color.

Balloons:
- 8
- 18
- 36 − 18
- 29
- 75 − 58
- 63 − 48
- 15
- 17
- 91 − 62
- 22 − 14

Scrambled Numbers

Where are the aliens hiding?
Solve the problems to spell the word.
Find the letter for each answer.
Write the matching letters on the lines below the problems.

| 5 = V   18 = E   14 = C   9 = A |

$$\begin{array}{r}120\\-106\\\hline\end{array}\qquad\begin{array}{r}118\\-109\\\hline\end{array}\qquad\begin{array}{r}112\\-107\\\hline\end{array}\qquad\begin{array}{r}120\\-102\\\hline\end{array}$$

____   ____   ____   ____

Alien Rescue!

Now the aliens want to leave the cave. Rocks are blocking the way. Solve the problems on the rocks.

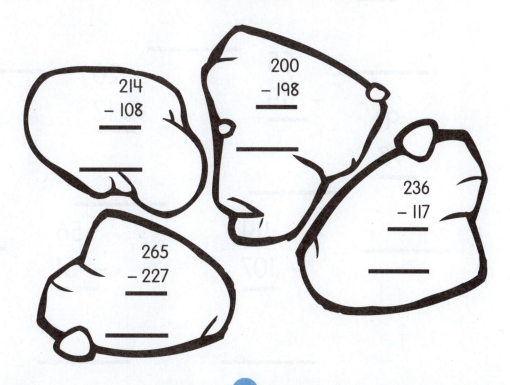

214 − 108 = ____

200 − 198 = ____

236 − 117 = ____

265 − 227 = ____

Guess the Problem

This is a game for two or more players.

Pick a problem, but don't tell anyone which one.

Solve the problem, and then clap, tap, jump, stomp, or blink that many times.

Can anyone guess which problem you solved?

Use the numbers on the next page if you need help.

```
   19        78        13
 - 16      - 63      -  4
 ____      ____      ____


            55        20
          - 49      - 12        25
   91     ____      ____      -  8
 - 78                         ____
 ____
            114       56
          - 107     - 51
          _____     ____
```

9

3

8

5

7

15

13

6

16

17

Count, Sort, Subtract

Create some interesting math chores that you can do as a family.

Fold the laundry together.

Put all the t-shirts, underwear, socks, or other like items together.

Count all the items in the group.

Take away one family member's items.

How many items are left?

Count, sort, and subtract silverware as you set the table. Take away the spoons. Now how many pieces of silverware are left?

Count, sort, and subtract toys as you put them away.

Count, sort, and subtract groceries as you put them away.

Count, sort, and subtract holiday gifts, photos, and anything else you can think of.

Note to Parents
Everyday chores, such as sorting laundry and setting the table, involve everyday math skills. One of the great benefits of involving children in household tasks is the practice they receive in classification, recognizing patterns, and simple arithmetic!

Matching Hats

Help the Ratini match his hats.

Solve each problem.

Draw a line from each problem to the correct answer.

Color the answer hat the same color as the matching problem.

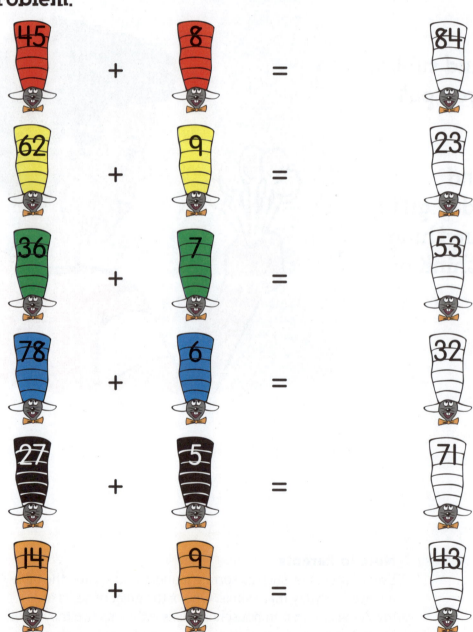

Alien Bowling!

It's time for alien bowling!

Solve each problem. Draw a line to the pin with the correct answer.

67 + 9 =

26 + 8 =

93 + 7 =

19 + 5 =

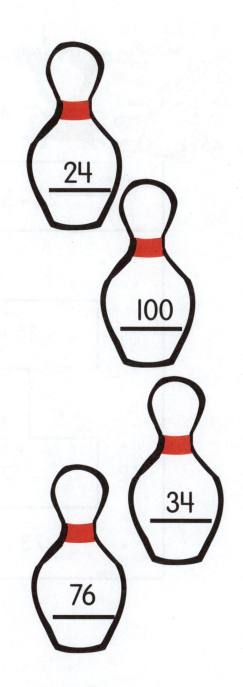

Add It Up

Two of these aliens ate all the cupcakes. Solve the problems on the path. Follow the path that has the correct answer after each problem.

Add in Space

Add 19 to each number in a red circle.
Write the answers in the blue spaces.

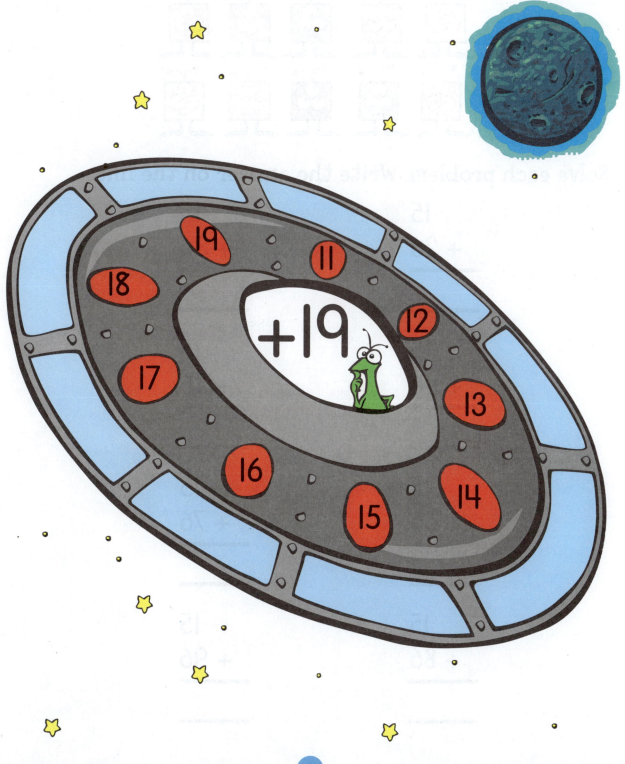

+15

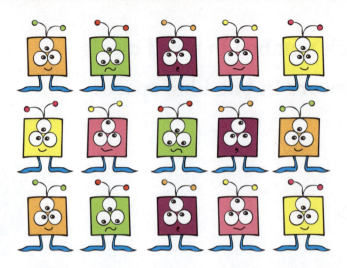

Solve each problem. Write the answer on the line.

```
   15            15
 + 26          + 36
 ____          ____

   15            15
 + 46          + 56
 ____          ____

   15            15
 + 66          + 76
 ____          ____

   15            15
 + 86          + 96
 ____          ____
```

Star Crossed

Solve each problem. Find the star that has the answer. Color the stars to match.

Counting Stars

Count the stars in each alien's hat.

How many stars are in the blue hat?

Fill in that number on the problems below. Then solve each problem.

How many stars are in the green hat?

Fill in that number on the problems on the next page.

Then solve each problem.

Write the sum on the line.

+ 37

+ 57

+ 77

+ 97

```
  + 27        + 67
  ____        ____


  + 37        + 77
  ____        ____


  + 47        + 87
  ____        ____


  + 57        + 97
  ____        ____
```

+101

Solve each problem. Write the answer on the line.

```
  101          101
+  19        +  29
-----        -----


  101          101
+  39        +  49
-----        -----


  101          101
+  59        +  69
-----        -----
```

Flower Fun

Help the alien color the flowers.
Solve each problem.
Match the answer to the key.
Then color the flower.

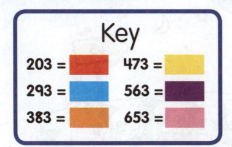

609 + 44

508 + 55

407 + 66

306 + 77

205 + 88

104 + 99

+505

Solve each problem.
Write the answer on the line.

```
  505        505        505
+ 103      + 206      + 308
-----      -----      -----


  505        505        505
+ 412      + 455      + 306
-----      -----      -----


             505        505
           + 377      + 458
           -----      -----
```

Shopping Trip

What do aliens spend when they shop in outer space?
To find out, solve each problem.
Then match the answers to the key.
Write the letters in order on the lines.

500	600	800	700	400
O	N	Y	E	M

1. 299
   + 101
   ─────

2. 299
   + 201
   ─────

3. 201
   + 299
   ─────

4. 299
   + 301
   ─────

5. 299
   + 401
   ─────

6. 299
   + 501
   ─────

__ __ __ __ __ __!
1. 2. 3. 4. 5. 6.

+909

Solve each problem.
Write the answer on the line.

```
  909          909          909
+ 111        + 232        + 343
_____        _____        _____


  909          909          909
+ 454        + 575        + 676
_____        _____        _____


               909          909
             + 781        + 816
             _____        _____
```

236

It's Puzzling

Solve each problem.

Draw lines to the puzzle pieces with the correct answers to finish the puzzle.

I did it!

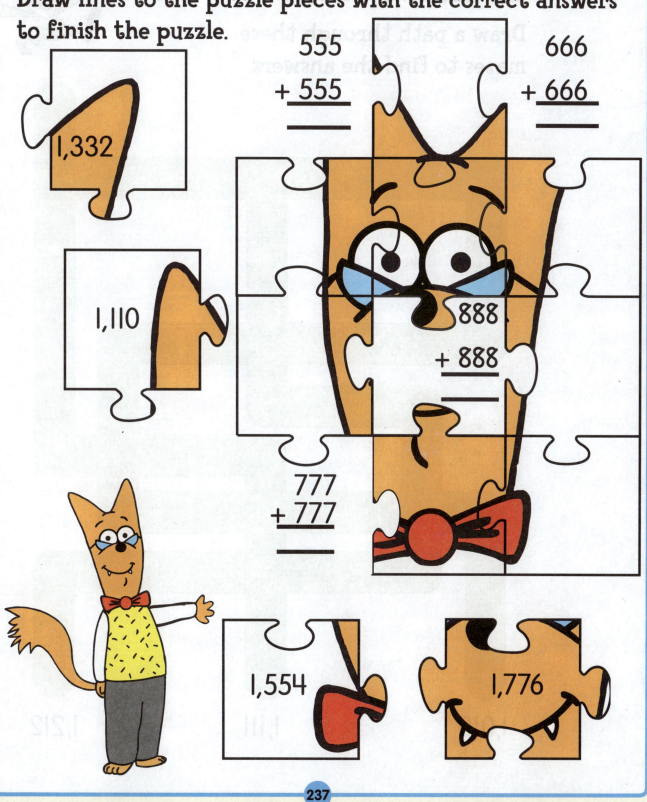

Mega Mazes

The aliens are trying to solve two different problems.

Draw a path through these mazes to find the answers.

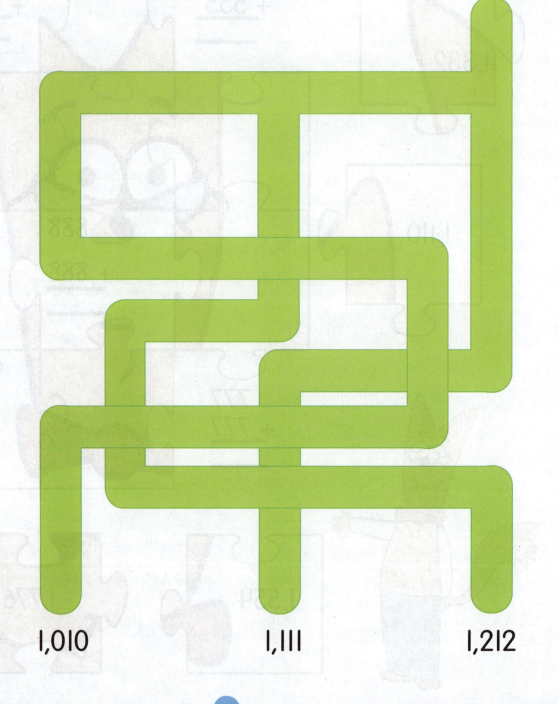

1,010 1,111 1,212

Stocking Up

Pop Fox owns a grocery store. Help him stock his shelves.

He already had 376 eggs. He got 137 more from the hen house. Now how many eggs does he have?

```
  376
+ 137
-----
```

Pop Fox has 225 apples at his store. How many will he have if he picks 176 more?

```
  225
+ 176
-----
```

Yesterday, Pop Fox ordered 116 bananas. Today, he ordered 55 more. How many bananas did he order in all?

```
  116
+  55
-----
```

STORY TIME

There were 127 boxes of cookies at the store. Pop Fox just got 65 more. How many boxes does he have now?

```
  127
+  65
-----
```

There were 198 jars of jam at the store. Pop Fox just got 224 more. How many does he have now?

```
  198
+ 224
-----
```

Pop Fox sells flowers too. He has 134 roses at the store. If he gets 99 more, how many will he have?

```
  134
+  99
-----
```

Pop Fox has everything he needs. He is all ready to open his store! Thanks for your help.

−8

Solve each problem. Write the answer on the line.

```
   11         22
 −  8       −  8
 ____       ____


   33         44
 −  8       −  8
 ____       ____


   55         66
 −  8       −  8
 ____       ____


   77         88
 −  8       −  8
 ____       ____
```

Kite Flight

Draw kite strings to the correct answers.
Color each alien to match its kite.

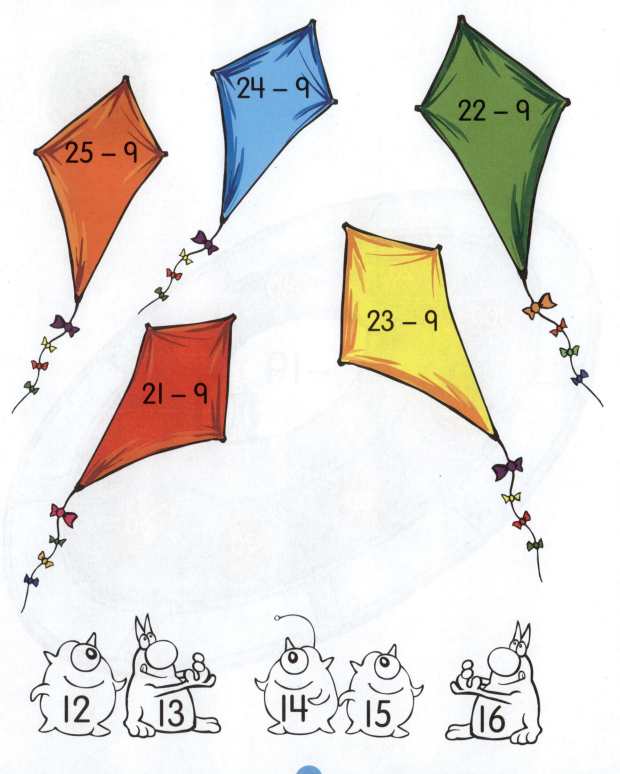

Subtract in Space

Subtract 19 from each number in a red space. Write the answers in the blue spaces.

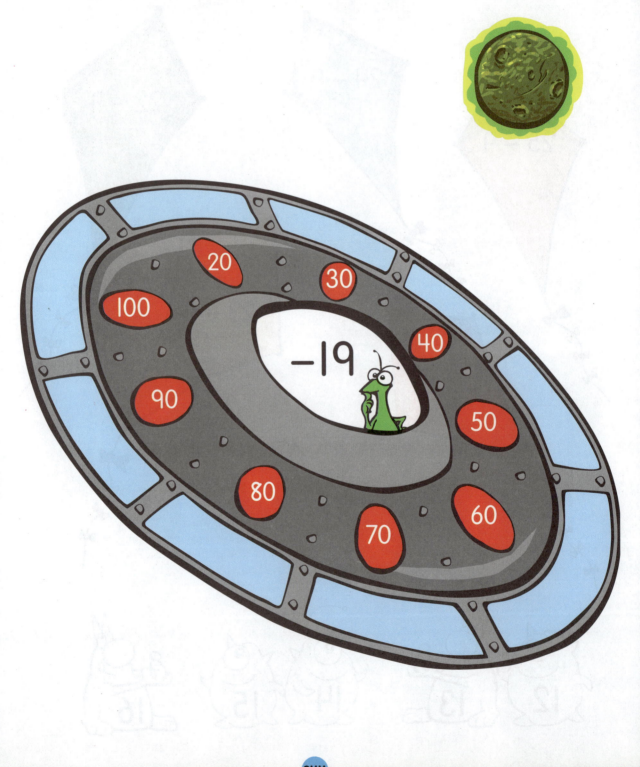

−55

Solve each problem. Write the answer on the line.

```
  101        120
 − 55       − 55
 ____       ____


  183        194
 − 55       − 55
 ____       ____


  201        262
 − 55       − 55
 ____       ____


  283        294
 − 55       − 55
 ____       ____
```

Boot Up

Solve each problem. Find the boot with the answer for each problem. Color the boot to match.

−777

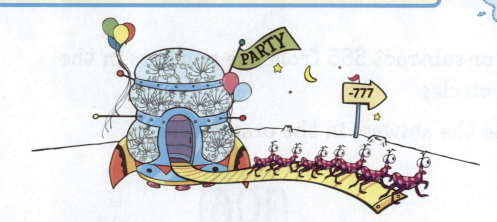

Solve each problem. Write the answer on the line.

$$\begin{array}{r}821\\-777\\\hline\end{array}\qquad\begin{array}{r}832\\-777\\\hline\end{array}$$

$$\begin{array}{r}848\\-777\\\hline\end{array}\qquad\begin{array}{r}859\\-777\\\hline\end{array}$$

$$\begin{array}{r}922\\-777\\\hline\end{array}\qquad\begin{array}{r}937\\-777\\\hline\end{array}$$

$$\begin{array}{r}946\\-777\\\hline\end{array}\qquad\begin{array}{r}952\\-777\\\hline\end{array}$$

Spin the Wheel

Add or subtract 555 from the numbers in the blue circles.

Write the answers in the orange wheel.

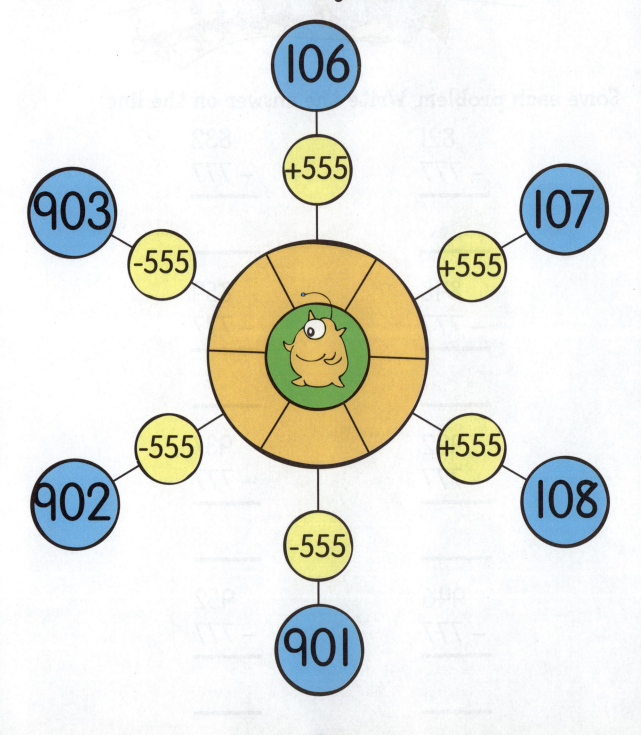

+ or − 909

Solve each problem. Write the answer on the line.

```
  115          161
+ 909        + 909
_____        _____

  178          351
+ 909        + 909
_____        _____

  923          945
− 909        − 909
_____        _____

  984        1,000
− 909        − 909
_____        _____
```

Loony Rover

Solve each problem. Match the answer to the key. Then color the rover.

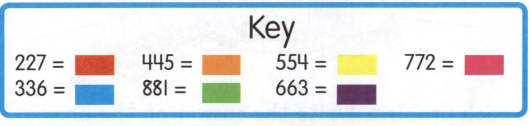

Key
227 = 🟥   445 = 🟧   554 = 🟨   772 = 🟪(pink)
336 = 🟦   881 = 🟩   663 = 🟪

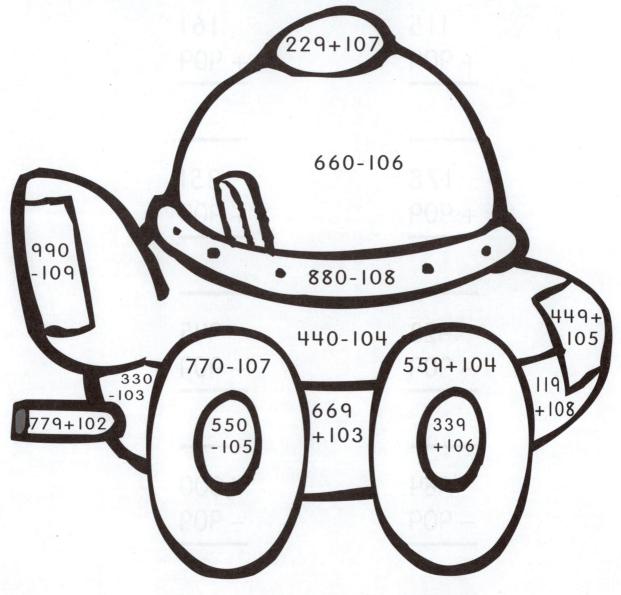

Ready, Set, Go!

I did it!

What sport do aliens like to watch? To find out, solve each problem. Then match the answers to the key. Write the letters in order on the lines.

```
  609        509        209        109        309
+ 189      + 189      + 189      + 189      + 189
_____      _____      _____      _____      _____


  800        600        500        700
- 202      - 202      - 202      - 202
_____      _____      _____      _____
```

Key

298	398	498	598	698	798
C	A	E	R	P	S

___ ___ ___ ___ ___

___ ___ ___

Back and Forth!

This game helps you check your subtraction.

Write each of the numbers and the signs from the next page on an index card.

Lay the cards out on the table exactly as you see them on the next page. Notice how each row shows a math problem and its answer. Look at the first problem. Is it correct?

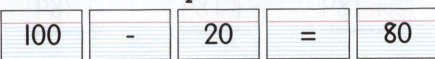

To check whether the answer is correct, reverse the order of the cards.

Replace the equal sign with an addition sign. Replace the subtraction sign with an equal sign. The problem should look like this:

If the answer to the new problem matches the first number of the old problem, the answer is correct.

100	-	20	=	80
1000	-	300	=	700
50	-	25	=	25
200	-	100	=	100
+	+	+	+	+

Answer Key

PAGE 196
2 + 1 = 3
1 + 3 = 4
4 + 2 = 6
5 + 1 = 6
3 + 2 = 5
4 + 1 = 5
2 + 4 = 6
5 + 2 = 7
4 + 3 = 7

PAGE 197
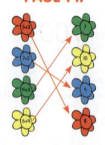

PAGE 198
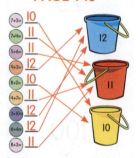

PAGE 199

PAGE 200
3 - 2 = 1
6 - 3 = 3
10 - 6 = 4

PAGE 201
10 - 2 = 8
12 - 6 = 6
8 - 8 = 0
11 - 2 = 9
6 - 3 = 3
12 - 7 = 5

PAGE 202
18 - 2 = 16
15 - 3 = 12
17 - 7 = 10

PAGE 203
16 - 5 = 11
18 - 7 = 11
17 - 8 = 9
10 - 4 = 6
16 - 7 = 9
14 - 8 = 6

PAGES 204-205
17 - 2 = 15
16 - 8 = 8
14 - 9 = 5
11 - 10 = 1
12 - 9 = 3
13 - 7 = 6
15 - 11 = 4
18 - 10 = 8

PAGE 208
14 + 12 = 26
19 + 11 = 30
15 + 10 = 25
13 + 12 = 25

PAGE 209
22 + 14 = 36
15 + 25 = 40
33 + 27 = 60

PAGE 210
44 + 27 = 71
53 + 38 = 91
55 + 26 = 81
67 + 18 = 85
79 + 16 = 95
84 + 17 = 101

PAGE 211
72 + 18 = 90
59 + 12 = 71
91 + 29 = 120
109 + 5 = 114

PAGES 212-213
28 + 33 = 61
66 + 18 = 84
45 + 9 = 54
99 + 14 = 113
85 + 29 = 114

PAGE 214

PAGE 215
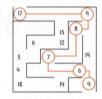

PAGE 216
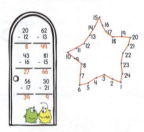

PAGE 217

PAGE 218
120 - 106 = 14
118 - 109 = 9
112 - 107 = 5
120 - 102 = 18
C - A - V - E

PAGE 219
214 - 108 = 106
265 - 227 = 38
200 - 198 = 2
236 - 117 = 119

PAGES 220-221
19 - 16 = 3
78 - 63 = 15
13 - 4 = 9
55 - 49 = 6
20 - 12 = 8
91 - 78 = 13
25 - 8 = 17
114 - 107 = 7
56 - 51 = 5

PAGE 224
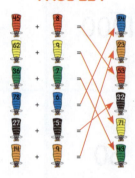

PAGE 225
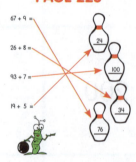

PAGE 226

PAGE 227
11 + 19 = 30
12 + 19 = 31
13 + 19 = 32
14 + 19 = 33
15 + 19 = 34
16 + 19 = 35
17 + 19 = 36
18 + 19 = 37
19 + 19 = 38

PAGE 228
15 + 26 = 41
15 + 36 = 51
15 + 46 = 61
15 + 56 = 71
15 + 66 = 81
15 + 76 = 91
15 + 86 = 101
15 + 96 = 111

PAGE 229

87 + 78 = 165
132
83 + 38 = 121
154
86 + 68 = 154
121
84 + 48 = 132
165

PAGE 230
14 + 37 = 51
14 + 57 = 71
14 + 77 = 91
14 + 97 = 111

PAGE 231
15 + 27 = 42
15 + 37 = 52
15 + 47 = 62
15 + 57 = 72
15 + 67 = 82
15 + 77 = 92
15 + 87 = 102
15 + 97 = 112

PAGE 232
101 + 19 = 120
101 + 29 = 130
101 + 39 = 140
101 + 49 = 150
101 + 59 = 160
101 + 69 = 170

PAGE 233

PAGE 234
505 + 103 = 608
505 + 206 = 711
505 + 308 = 813
505 + 412 = 917
505 + 455 = 960
505 + 306 = 811
505 + 377 = 882
505 + 458 = 963

PAGE 235
299 + 101 = 400
299 + 201 = 500
201 + 299 = 500
299 + 301 = 600
299 + 401 = 700
299 + 501 = 800
M-O-O-N-E-Y!

PAGE 236
909 + 111 = 1,020
909 + 232 = 1,141
909 + 343 = 1,252
909 + 454 = 1,363
909 + 575 = 1,484
909 + 676 = 1,585
909 + 781 = 1,690
909 + 816 = 1,725

PAGE 237
555 + 555 = 1,110
666 + 666 = 1,332
777 + 777 = 1,554
888 + 888 = 1,776

PAGES 238–239
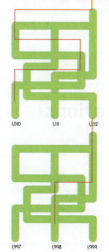

PAGES 240–241
376 + 137 = 513
225 + 176 = 401
116 + 55 = 171

PAGE 241
127 + 65 = 192
198 + 224 = 422
134 + 99 = 233

PAGE 242
11 - 8 = 3
22 - 8 = 14
33 - 8 = 25
44 - 8 = 36
55 - 8 = 47
66 - 8 = 58
77 - 8 = 69
88 - 8 = 80

PAGE 243

PAGE 244
20 - 19 = 1
30 - 19 = 11
40 - 19 = 21
50 - 19 = 31
60 - 19 = 41
70 - 19 = 51
80 - 19 = 61
90 - 19 = 71
100 - 19 = 81

PAGE 245
101 - 55 = 46
120 - 55 = 65
183 - 55 = 128
194 - 55 = 139
201 - 55 = 146
262 - 55 = 207
283 - 55 = 228
294 - 55 = 239

PAGE 246

PAGE 247
821 - 777 = 44
832 - 777 = 55
848 - 777 = 71
859 - 777 = 82
922 - 777 = 145
937 - 777 = 160
946 - 777 = 169
952 - 777 = 175

PAGE 248
555 + 106 = 661
555 + 107 = 662
555 + 108 = 663
901 - 555 = 346
902 - 555 = 347
903 - 555 = 348

PAGE 249
115 + 909 = 1,024
161 + 909 = 1,070
178 + 909 = 1,087
351 + 909 = 1,260
923 - 909 = 14
945 - 909 = 36
984 - 909 = 75
1000 - 909 = 91

PAGE 250

PAGE 251
609 + 189 = 798
509 + 189 = 698
209 + 189 = 398
109 + 189 = 298
309 + 189 = 498
800 - 202 = 598
600 - 202 = 398
500 - 202 = 298
700 - 202 = 498
S-P-A-C-E
R-A-C-E

PAGE 253

100	-	20	=	80
1000	-	300	=	700
50	-	25	=	25
200	-	100	=	100
+	+	+	+	+

I did it!

Congratulations!

_____

has successfully completed this workbook.

2nd Grade

Hooked on Math®

Time, Money, and Fractions

Copyright © 2007 Educate Products, LLC. All rights reserved.
Printed in China. No part of this publication may be reproduced, stored in any retrieval system or transmitted, in any form or by any means, electronic, mechanical, photocopying, recording, or otherwise, without the prior written permission of the publisher.

50 Is Nifty!

Can you count to 50? Can you show me how?
Now count to 50. Then take a bow!

Skip Count Now

Count by 2s. Please do it now.

Count by 5s. Please show me how.

Count by 10s. Please take a bow!

1	2	3	4	5	6	7	8	9	10
11	12	13	14	15	16	17	18	19	20
21	22	23	24	25	26	27	28	29	30
31	32	33	34	35	36	37	38	39	40
41	42	43	44	45	46	47	48	49	50
51	52	53	54	55	56	57	58	59	60
61	62	63	64	65	66	67	68	69	70
71	72	73	74	75	76	77	78	79	80
81	82	83	84	85	86	87	88	89	90
91	92	93	94	95	96	97	98	99	100

Pizza Power!

Look at the pizzas. Both are cut into two parts. Only one is cut into two parts that are the same size, or equal.

Equal Parts   Not Equal Parts

Find pizzas that are cut into equal parts. Circle them.

Are They Equal?

Color the shapes that have equal parts.

Draw, Color, and Share

The alien says there are two equal parts.
Each part is $\frac{1}{2}$ of the whole.

Draw a line on each treat to show equal halves.
Color $\frac{1}{2}$ of each treat.
Share your treats with a friend!

Which Are Equal?

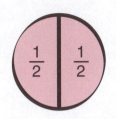 

There are two equal parts. Each part is $\frac{1}{2}$.

There are three equal parts. Each part is $\frac{1}{3}$.

Circle each shape that shows halves.

 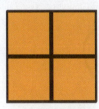  

Circle each shape that shows thirds.

Color with the Aliens!

These aliens want to color!

Color $\frac{1}{2}$ of each shape red.

Color $\frac{1}{3}$ of each shape green.

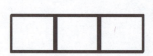

Color $\frac{1}{4}$ of each shape blue.

What Part Is Blue?

There are three aliens in this group. One alien is blue. $\frac{1}{3}$ of the group is blue.

What part of each group is blue? Circle the fraction.

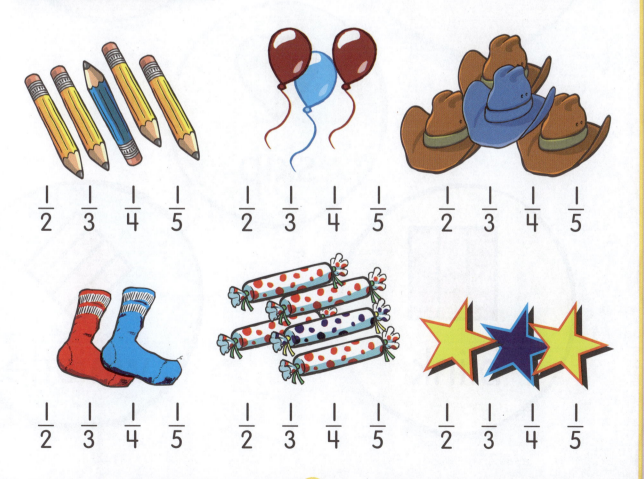

$\frac{1}{2}$ $\frac{1}{3}$ $\frac{1}{4}$ $\frac{1}{5}$ $\frac{1}{2}$ $\frac{1}{3}$ $\frac{1}{4}$ $\frac{1}{5}$ $\frac{1}{2}$ $\frac{1}{3}$ $\frac{1}{4}$ $\frac{1}{5}$

$\frac{1}{2}$ $\frac{1}{3}$ $\frac{1}{4}$ $\frac{1}{5}$ $\frac{1}{2}$ $\frac{1}{3}$ $\frac{1}{4}$ $\frac{1}{5}$ $\frac{1}{2}$ $\frac{1}{3}$ $\frac{1}{4}$ $\frac{1}{5}$

Count and Act It Out

Toss a coin onto these two pages. In which circle did it land? Look at the shape inside the circle. Count its equal parts. Skip, blink, clap, whistle, or twirl that many times!

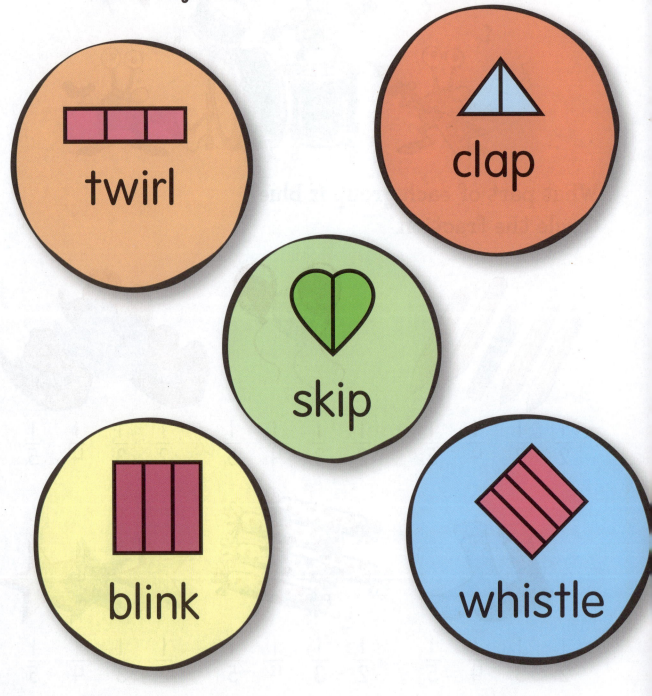

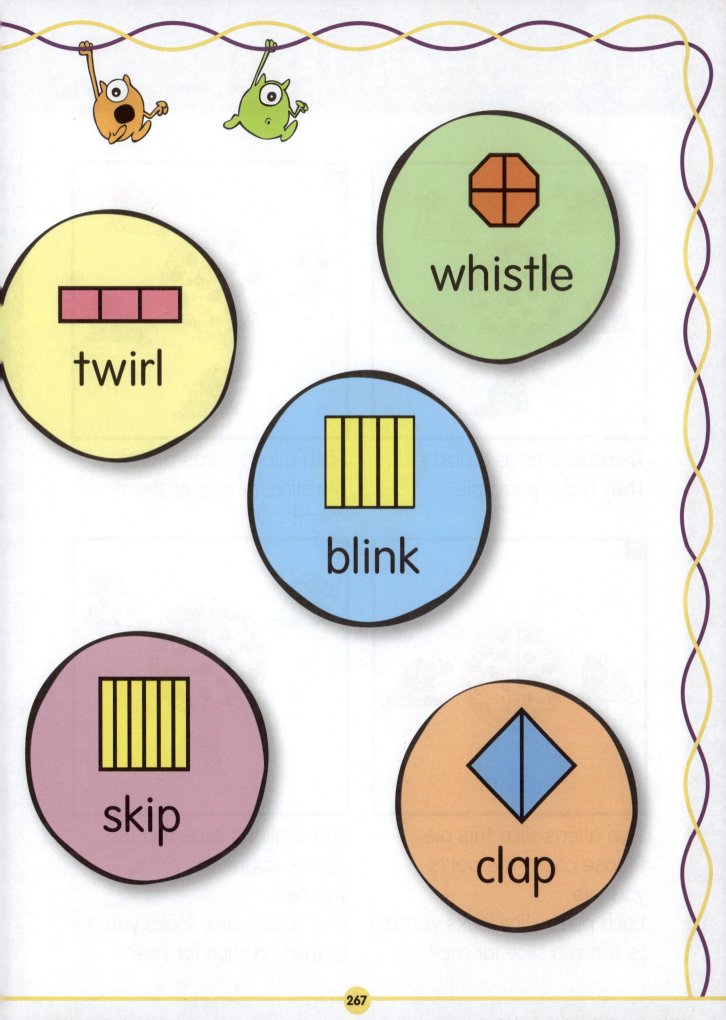

Party On, Aliens!

The aliens have a party.
They order pizza pie.

Each alien wants a nice
big slice, or one of them
might cry!

Two aliens slice this pie.
Please count the parts
you see.
Each pizza slice looks yummy.
Is there a slice for me?

Three aliens slice this pie.
Please count the parts
you see.
Each pizza slice looks yummy.
Is there a slice for me?

Four aliens slice this pie.
Please count the parts
you see.
Each pizza slice looks yummy.
Is there a slice for me?

Five aliens slice this pie.
Please count the parts
you see.
Each pizza slice looks yummy.
Is there a slice for me?

Five aliens slice this pie.
Please count the parts
you see.

Each pizza slice looks yummy.
They cut one slice for me!

What Part Is Green?

There are six aliens in this group.

One alien is green.

$\frac{1}{6}$ of the group is green.

$\frac{5}{6}$ of the group is red.

Look at the aliens. What part of the group is green? What part of the group is red? Write each fraction.

1.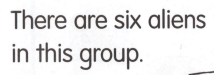

___ is green.

___ is red.

2.

___ is green.

___ is red.

3.

___ is green.

___ is red.

4.

___ is green.

___ is red.

5.

___ are green.

___ is red.

6.

___ is green.

___ is red.

Color Us!

There are seven aliens in this group.

One alien is blue.

$\frac{1}{7}$ of the group is blue.

$\frac{6}{7}$ of the group is red.

Color one alien blue in each box.

Color the rest red in each box.

Write each fraction.

1. How many are blue? $\frac{1}{7}$	2. How many are red? ____	3. How many are blue? ____
4. How many are red? ____	5. How many are blue? ____	6. How many are red? ____

Presents, Please

What fraction of each group of presents is red? Draw a line from each alien's sign to the correct picture.

Alien Fractions

There are nine aliens in this group.

One alien is red.

$\frac{1}{9}$ of the group is red.

$\frac{8}{9}$ of the group is green.

Count the aliens in each box. Write each fraction to answer the question.

1. How many are red? $\frac{2}{9}$	2. How many are green? ____	3. How many are red? ____
4. How many are green? ____	5. How many are red? ____	6. How many are green? ____

Find the Spaceships

This alien needs help! What fraction of each group of spaceships is red?

Draw a line from the fraction to the correct answer.

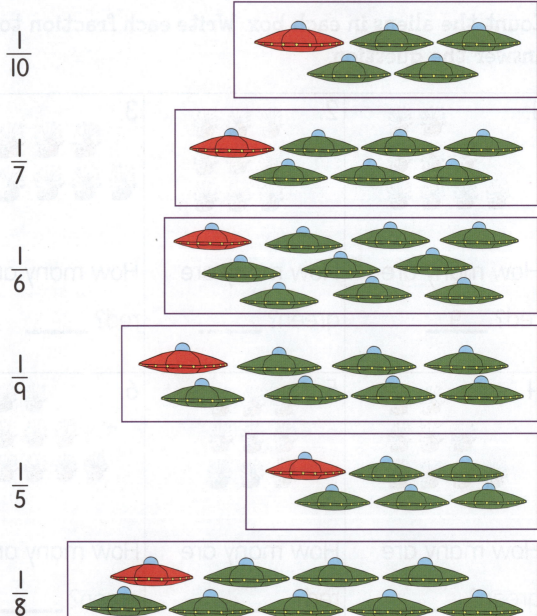

These Aliens Rock!

What fraction of the things in each box are blue?

1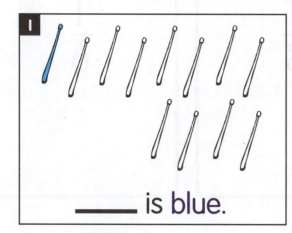
____ is blue.

2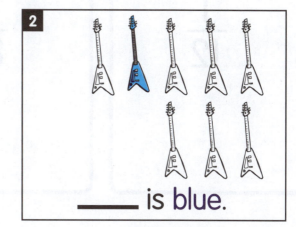
____ is blue.

3
____ is blue.

4
____ is blue.

Find and Match

What fraction of each group of aliens is red?

Draw a line from each fraction to the matching group of aliens on the next page.

$\frac{1}{12}$

$\frac{1}{8}$

$\frac{1}{6}$

$\frac{1}{9}$

$\frac{1}{7}$

$\frac{1}{10}$

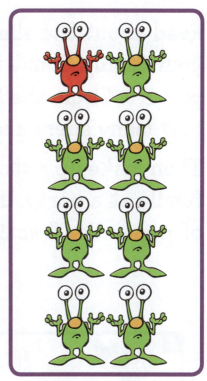

Come to the Party!

Read about the aliens' party with your family. Count the aliens in each picture. Circle the fraction that shows how many aliens are sick.

Then make up a story about your family at a party. Use a separate sheet of paper. Use fractions in your story.

The aliens have a party, but one of them is sick. Count the aliens that you see. What fraction do you pick?

The aliens have some cupcakes, but one of them is sick. Count the aliens that you see. What fraction do you pick?

$\frac{1}{6}$ $\frac{1}{12}$ $\frac{1}{3}$

$\frac{1}{7}$ $\frac{1}{8}$ $\frac{1}{9}$

The aliens have some candy, but one of them is sick. Count the aliens that you see. What fraction do you pick?

$\frac{1}{3}$ $\frac{1}{2}$ $\frac{1}{10}$

The aliens have some ice cream, but one of them is sick. Count the aliens that you see. What fraction do you pick?

$\frac{1}{9}$ $\frac{1}{8}$ $\frac{1}{10}$

Note to Parents
Use the Family Fun activity below as a guide in making up a new story with your child. Encourage your child to illustrate the story. Include a line about fractions so that your child can practice them.

There are five people in my family.
Let's give ourselves a cheer!
One of us plays baseball.
Write the fraction here: $\frac{1}{5}$

There are five people in my family.
Let's give ourselves a cheer!
Two of us like apples.
Write the fraction here: $\frac{2}{5}$

Time to Tell Time!

The long hand is the minute hand.
The short hand is the hour hand.
What time does the alien wake up?

7:00

1.
___:___

2.
___:___

3.
___:___

4.
___:___

5.
___:___

6.

Now try this!
The alien goes to bed at 8:00.
Draw the hour hand.

Alien Times

Read about the alien's day.
Draw the hour hand on each clock to show what time the alien did each thing.

1.
breakfast at 8:00

2.
make bed at 9:00

3.
play at 10:00

4.
lunch at 12:00

5.
nap at 1:00

6.
snack at 3:00

7.
play at 4:00

8.
dinner at 6:00

9.
bath at 7:00

What Time Is It?

The aliens walk to school at 8:30. The clock shows 8:30 when the hour hand is between 8 and 9, and the minute hand points to 6.

Look at the clocks below.
Write the time on the line below each clock.

1.

2.

3.

___ : ___   ___ : ___   ___ : ___

4.

5.

6.

___ : ___   ___ : ___   ___ : ___

Draw the Time!

The alien climbs on the monkey bars at 3:30. The clock shows 3:30 when the hour is between 3 and 4, and the minute hand points to 6.

Draw the hour hand on each clock to show what time it is.

1.
It is 4:30.

2.
It is 1:30.

3.
It is 11:30.

4.
It is 6:30.

5.
It is 12:30.

6.
It is 5:30.

Find It!

Help the alien tell time.
Draw lines between the clocks that show the same time.

Draw and Write!

On the lines in each box, write the time shown on the clock on the left. Then draw the time on the other clock.

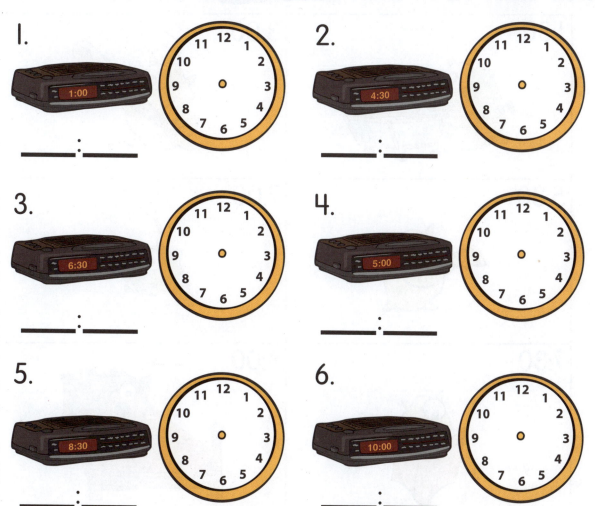

Act It Out

Play this game with a friend.
Take turns reading the times below.

Look at what the alien is doing.
Act out the activity.

Then find the clock with the correct time on the next page.

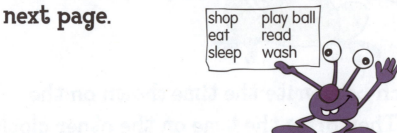

shop play ball
eat   read
sleep wash

1:30

3:00

5:30

7:00

7:30

8:00

The Alien Race

Read the story. At what time does each part happen?

1.
It is time for the alien to run in a race.

___ : ___

2.
The alien runs at a very fast pace!

___ : ___

3.
He runs along a rocky road.

___ : ___

4.
He passes one gigantic toad.

___ : ___

5.

The alien stops to take a break.

____ : ____

6.

Then he sees a great big lake.

____ : ____

7.

The alien comes to the end of the race.

____ : ____

8.

Shout hooray! He won the race!

____ : ____

Count by 5s

There are five minutes between each number on the clock. Count by 5s to find the minutes after the hour. Write the minutes and the hours shown on the clocks.

__5__ minutes after __8__

____ minutes after ____

____ minutes after ____

____ minutes after ____

____ minutes after ____

____ minutes after ____

Draw the Hands!

This alien needs help! Draw the clock's hands. Then write the minutes and the hours shown on the clocks.

_____ minutes after _____

_____ minutes after _____

_____ minutes after _____   _____ minutes after _____

_____ minutes after _____

_____ minutes after _____

Count by 10s

The aliens play a new song every 10 minutes. There are 10 minutes between the 12 and the 2. Count by 10s to find the minutes after the hour. Then write the minutes and the hours shown on the clocks.

____ minutes after ____

____ minutes after ____   ____ minutes after ____

____ minutes after ____   ____ minutes after ____

Match the Times

Help this alien match the times.
Find the matching times in each column.
Draw lines to connect them.

40 minutes after 10

10 minutes after 1

20 minutes after 9

30 minutes after 11

50 minutes after 7

Boo-hoo, Wah-wah!

The baby alien wakes up every 15 minutes. Look at each clock. Write the hour and the minutes.

hour____ minutes____

hour____ minutes____   hour____ minutes____

hour____ minutes____   hour____ minutes____

Time for a Race!

These aliens have run a race. The clocks show the different times that each alien finished. Write the time on the lines.

___ : ___   ___ : ___   ___ : ___

___ : ___   ___ : ___   ___ : ___

___ : ___   ___ : ___   ___ : ___

The Action Clock Game

This is a game for two or more players.

How to play:

1. The first player picks a clock and acts out the word written below it.

2. The other players guess which clock the player has chosen by calling out the time on the clock above the word.

3. Keep taking turns until all the times have been guessed.

sniff

sing

skip

hop

Saturday Is Fun Day

Think of fun activities you like to do on Saturdays. Write a sentence about each activity and then draw hands on the clocks to show what time you do the activity.

I _____   I _____

Note to Parents
Throughout the day, encourage your child to tell time by asking questions, such as "We need to go to Grandma's at 10:00. What time is it now?" *or* "Soccer practice is at 3:30. We need to leave at 3:15. Would you remind me?" *or* "Would you set the table at 5:00? Thanks!"

I _____

I _____

I _____

I _____

I _____

I _____

Let's Count!

Pennies are worth one cent. Nickels are worth five cents. How much is each group of coins worth?

One nickel equals $0.05.   One penny equals $0.01.

1. $0.____ in all

2. $0.____ in all

3. $0.____ in all

4. $0.____ in all

Hugo has four nickels and three pennies. How much are his coins worth? $0.____

Can he buy the pail? _____

$0.22

The Price Is Right

Each of these things has a price. Circle the coins that add up to each price.

One dime equals ten pennies.
One dime equals two nickels.
One dime equals $0.10.

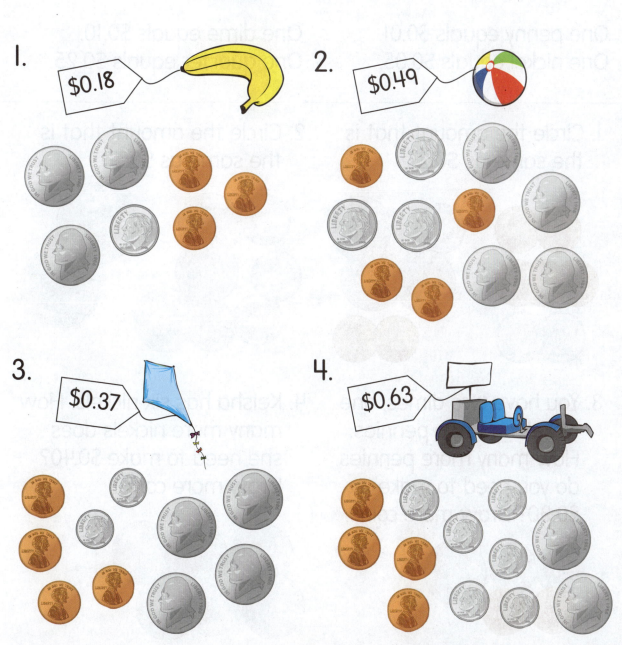

1. $0.18

2. $0.49

3. $0.37

4. $0.63

Count and Add

Read and solve each problem.

One penny equals $0.01. One dime equals $0.10.
One nickel equals $0.05. One quarter equals $0.25.

1. Circle the amount that is the same as $0.25.

2. Circle the amount that is the same as $0.50.

3. You have two dimes, one nickel, and two pennies. How many more pennies do you need to make $0.30? Draw more coins.

4. Keisha has six nickels. How many more nickels does she need to make $0.40? Draw more coins.

Time for Change

It's time to make change!
If you pay for these things with the coins shown, how much money will you get back? Write the amount of your change on the line.

price	you pay	your change
hat $0.18	dime, dime	_____
soda $0.24	quarter	_____
pen $0.32	quarter, dime	_____
pizza $0.46	quarter, dime, dime, nickel	_____

Dollar Cents!

Add up the value of the coins.
Write each amount in cents.
Draw more coins to make
the total add up to one dollar.

One hundred pennies equals $1.00.

1.

   _____

2.

   _____

3.

   _____

Write each amount in cents.
Circle the group that adds up to one dollar.

4.

   _____

5.

   _____

6.

   _____

Match It

Draw lines to match each thing to the amount of money it costs.

Add and Act

This is a game for two players.

You will need:
a button

Play this game with a friend. Throw a button on the page. Add up the group of coins the button lands on, and find a toy that costs that amount on the next page. Pretend to play with it. Can your friend guess which toy you picked?

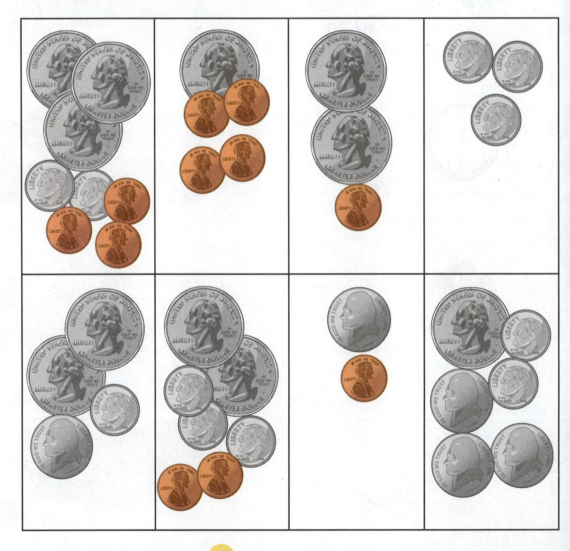

Let's Buy a Toy

Count the money.
Which toy costs that amount?
Circle the correct answer.

Count the money that you see.
Then choose a toy to buy.
Be sure you have the money.
Just add. Give it a try!

Count the money that you see.
Which airplane can you buy?
Be sure you have the money.
Just add. Give it a try!

Count the money that you see.
Which bracelet can you buy?
Be sure you have the money.
Just add. Give it a try!

Count the money that you see.
Which drum can you buy?
Be sure you have the money.
Just add. Give it a try!

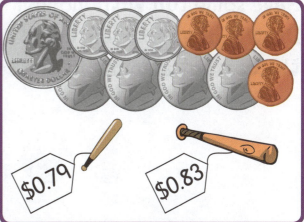

Count the money that you see.
Which helmet can you buy?
Be sure you have the money.
Just add. Give it a try!

Count the money that you see.
Which bat can you buy?
Be sure you have the money.
Just add. Give it a try!

Count the money that you see.
Which teddy can you buy?
Be sure you have the money.
Just add. Give it a try!

Count the money that you see.
Which doll can you buy?
Be sure you have the money.
Just add. Give it a try!

Note to Parents
Help your child learn about handling money. For example, when you go grocery shopping, count the change you receive together. At the gas station, encourage your child to read how much each type of gas costs. Finally, play addition and subtraction games together using money.

Match the Amounts

Have some fun with money! Draw a line from the coins to the correct amount in the second column.

(2 nickels)	$0.06
(1 dime, 1 nickel, 4 pennies)	$0.48
(6 nickels, 2 pennies)	$1.00
(1 quarter, 2 dimes, 3 pennies)	$0.27
(1 nickel, 8 dimes, 1 penny)	$0.76
(1 nickel, 1 penny)	$0.19
(4 quarters)	$0.10

Adding Coins

Circle the coins you need to buy each item.

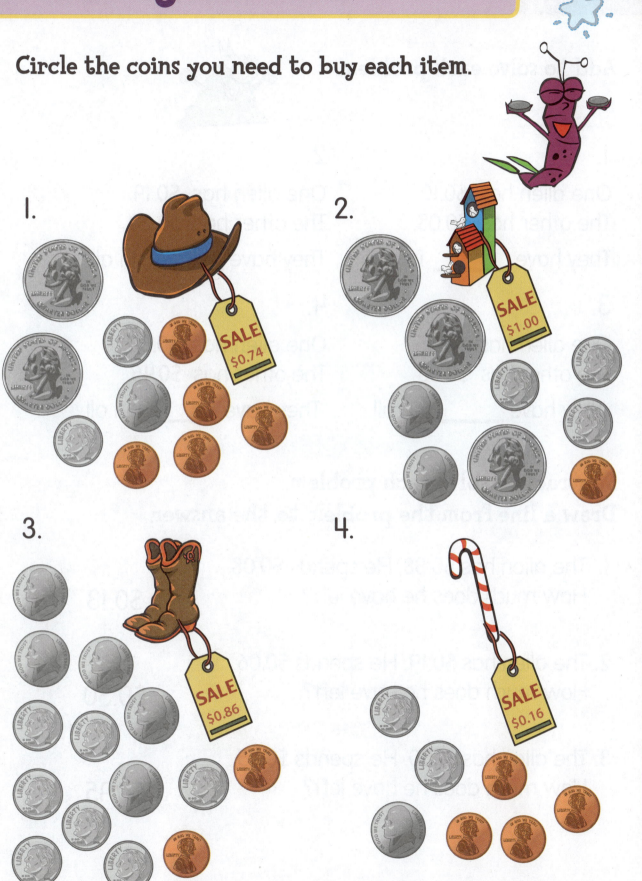

How Much Money?

Add to solve each problem.

1. One alien has $0.10.
The other has $0.08.
They have _____ in all.

2. One alien has $0.19.
The other has $0.20.
They have _____ in all.

3. One alien has $0.35.
The other has $0.03.
They have _____ in all.

4. One alien has $0.50.
The other has $0.45.
They have _____ in all.

**Subtract to solve each problem.
Draw a line from the problem to the answer.**

1. The alien has $0.38. He spends $0.08.
How much does he have left?

    $0.13

2. The alien has $0.19. He spends $0.06.
How much does he have left?

    $0.30

3. The alien has $1.00. He spends $0.05.
How much does he have left?

    $0.95

Add and Draw

You know that 100 pennies equals $1.00. Count the money. Draw coins to make the total add up to $1.00.

1.

2.

3.

4.

5.

6.

7. Draw coins to make $1.00 in another way.

Count On!

Help this alien add up his coins one by one. As you add each coin, write the new total on the line below it.

Example:

$0.25 $0.50 $0.60 $0.65 $0.66   Total: $0.66

1.

_____ _____ _____ _____ _____   Total: _____

2.

_____ _____ _____ _____ _____   Total: _____

3.

_____ _____ _____ _____ _____   Total: _____

4.

_____ _____ _____ _____ _____   Total: _____

How Much Change?

The alien goes food shopping. Help him figure out how much change he should get.

Food	Price	The alien has this much money.	How much change will he get?
	$0.43	$0.50	$0.07
	$0.96	$1.00	_____
	$0.74	$0.75	_____
	$0.63	$0.65	_____
	$0.17	$0.20	_____
	$0.88	$0.95	_____

What's in a Name?

Write your first and last name on a piece of paper. Find the value of each letter below. Add the value of the letters. How much is your name worth? How much is each alien's name worth? Figure it out!

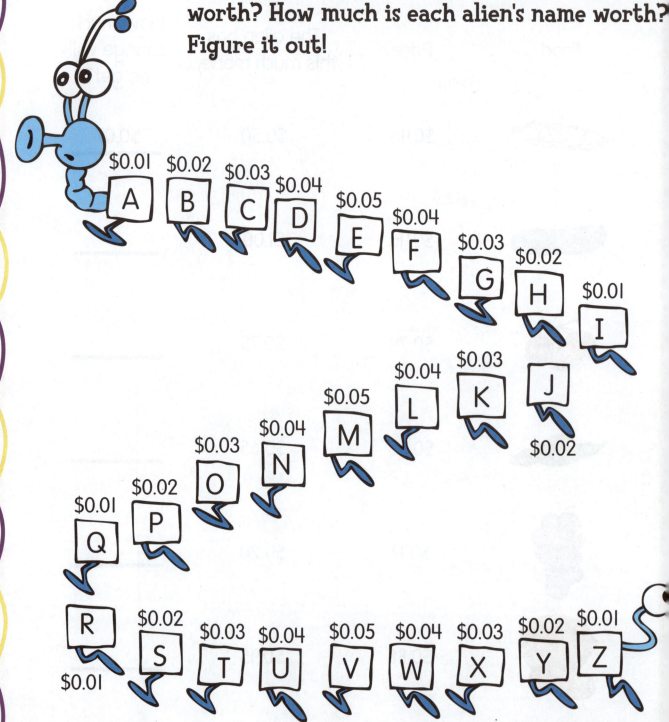

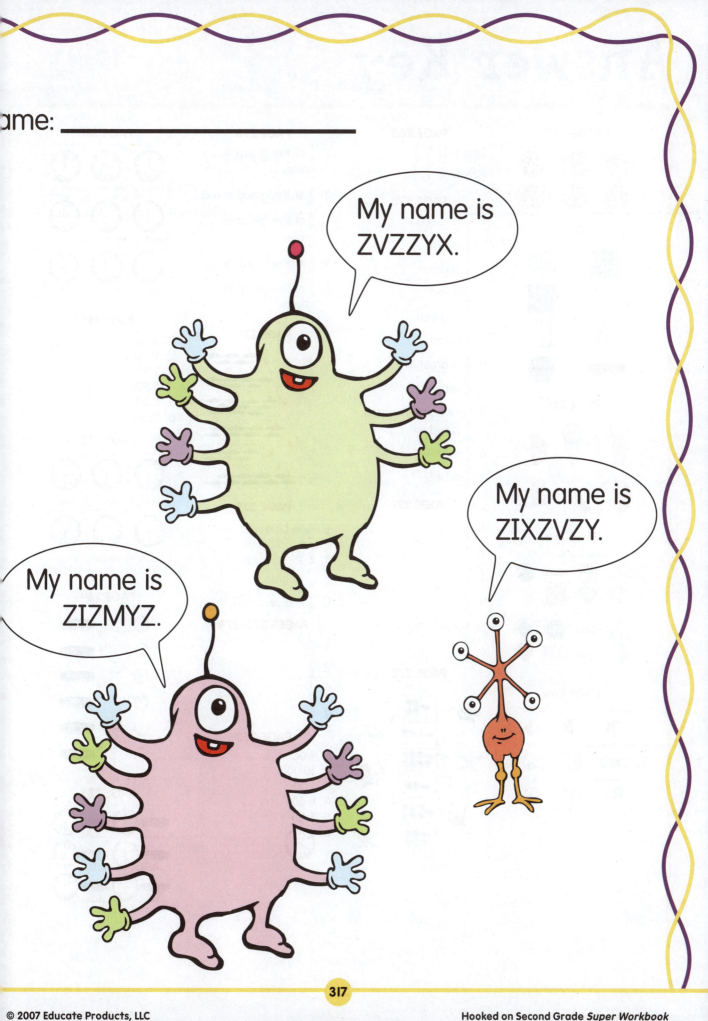

Answer Key

PAGE 260

PAGE 261

PAGE 262

PAGE 263

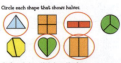
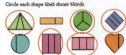

PAGE 264

PAGE 265

Row 1: $\frac{1}{5}, \frac{1}{3}, \frac{1}{4}$
Row 2: $\frac{1}{2}, \frac{1}{5}, \frac{1}{3}$

PAGE 270

1. $\frac{1}{2}$ is green.
   $\frac{1}{2}$ is red.
2. $\frac{1}{4}$ is green.
   $\frac{3}{4}$ is red.
3. $\frac{1}{6}$ is green.
   $\frac{5}{6}$ is red.
4. $\frac{1}{3}$ is green.
   $\frac{2}{3}$ is red.
5. 0 (or none) is green.
   $\frac{6}{6}$ is red.
6. $\frac{1}{5}$ is green.
   $\frac{4}{5}$ is red.

PAGE 271

1. $\frac{1}{7}$
2. $\frac{1}{2}$
3. $\frac{1}{5}$
4. $\frac{2}{3}$
5. $\frac{1}{6}$
6. $\frac{3}{4}$

PAGE 272

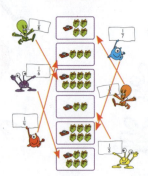

PAGE 273

2. $\frac{6}{9}$ of the group is green.
3. $\frac{4}{9}$ of the group is red.
4. $\frac{4}{9}$ of the group is green.
5. $\frac{6}{9}$ of the group is red.
6. $\frac{2}{9}$ of the group is green.

PAGE 274

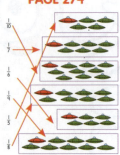

PAGE 275

1. $\frac{1}{12}$ is blue.
2. $\frac{1}{8}$ is blue.
3. $\frac{1}{10}$ is blue.
4. $\frac{1}{9}$ is blue.

PAGES 278–279

1. $\frac{1}{12}$
2. $\frac{1}{8}$
3. $\frac{1}{3}$
4. $\frac{1}{9}$

PAGE 280

1. 8:00
2. 10:00
3. 1:00
4. 4:00
5. 5:00
6.

PAGE 281

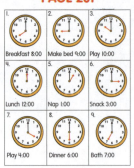

PAGE 282

1. 9:30
2. 11:30
3. 2:30
4. 5:30
5. 3:30
6. 10:30

PAGE 283

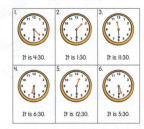

PAGE 284

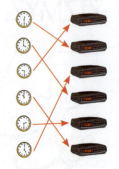

PAGE 285

Hooked on Second Grade *Super Workbook* © 2007 Educate Products, LLC

PAGES 288–289
1. 9:30
2. 10:00
3. 10:30
4. 11:00
5. 11:30
6. 12:00
7. 12:30
8. 1:00

PAGE 290
Row 1: 10 minutes after 8:00

Row 2: 25 minutes after 3:00; 15 minutes after 10:00

Row 3: 40 minutes after 9:00; 30 minutes after 7:00

PAGE 291

PAGE 292
Row 1: 10 minutes after 11:00

Row 2: 30 minutes after 4:00; 40 minutes after 1:00

Row 3: 20 minutes after 7:00; 50 minutes after 3:00

PAGE 293
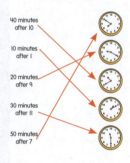

PAGE 294
Row 1: 12:15

Row 2: 3:45; 9:30

Row 3: 7:30; 2:15

PAGE 295
Row 1: 8:15; 8:30; 8:45

Row 2: 3:30; 3:45; 4:00

Row 3: 10:45; 11:00; 11:15

PAGE 300
1. $0.08
2. $0.20
3. $0.19
4. $0.27

Hugo has $0.23. Yes, he has $0.01 more than the price of the pail.

PAGE 301
Answers will vary. Possible answers:
1. 3 nickels, 3 pennies
2. 3 dimes, 3 nickels, 4 pennies
3. 2 dimes, 3 nickels, 2 pennies
4. 6 dimes, 3 pennies

PAGE 302

3 pennies   2 nickels

PAGE 303
Row 1: $0.02

Row 2: $0.01

Row 3: $0.03

Row 4: $0.04

PAGE 304
1. $0.75; possible answer: draw one more quarter
2. $0.80; possible answer: draw two more dimes
3. $0.90; possible answer: draw two more nickels
4. $0.95
5. $0.98
6. $1.00 (circle)

PAGE 305
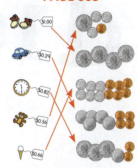

PAGE 306
Row 1: $0.98; $0.29; $0.51; $0.30

Row 2: $0.65; $0.82; $0.06; $0.60

PAGE 308
Row 1: You can buy the airplane for $0.70.

Row 2: You can buy the bracelet for $0.63. You can buy the drum for $0.45.

PAGE 309
Row 1: You can buy the helmet for $0.95. You can buy the bat for $0.79.

Row 2: You can buy the teddy for $0.57. You can buy the buy the doll for $0.42.

PAGE 310
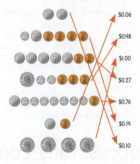

PAGE 311

PAGE 312
1. $0.18
2. $0.39
3. $0.38
4. $0.95

1. $0.30
2. $0.13
3. $0.95

PAGE 313
1. one quarter
2. three dimes
3. one dime
4. two dimes
5. one quarter or two dimes and one nickel
6. two dimes

PAGE 314
1. $0.25, $0.35, $0.45, $0.50, $0.55, Total: $0.55
2. $0.25, $0.50, $0.75, $0.85, $0.86, Total: $0.86
3. $0.25, $0.30, $0.35, $0.36, $0.37, Total: $0.37
4. $0.25, $0.35, $0.45, $0.55, $0.65, Total: $0.65

PAGE 315
cucumber—$0.04

cherries—$0.01

beans—$0.02

grapes—$0.03

nuts—$0.07

I did it!

Congratulations!

_____

_____

has successfully completed this workbook.